THE ROCKEFELLER FAMILY HOME
KYKUIT

Photographs by Mary Louise Pierson
Text by Ann Rockefeller Roberts
Captions and additional text by Cynthia Altman

Abbeville Press   Publishers   New York   London   Paris

In memory of
LAURA AND JOHN D. ROCKEFELLER SR. *and*
ABBY AND JOHN D. ROCKEFELLER JR.

Jacket front: View of Kykuit from the east (see also p. 60).

Jacket back, top left: The brook garden (see also p. 150). Top right: The dining room (see also p. 76). Bottom left: The swimming pool in the Playhouse (see also p. 128). Bottom right: Aristide Maillol's Bather Putting Up Her Hair, *1930 (see also p. 176). Center: John D. Rockefeller Sr. (center), John D. Rockefeller Jr. (left), and Nelson Rockefeller, holding his son Rodman on the porch at Kykuit (see also p. 8).*

Half-title page: View of forecourt from the south porch of the Big House.

Title spread: An ogikata-style stone lantern sits on a small peninsula of white stones in the Japanese garden.

This page: Detail of the lantern and elaborate ironwork above the passage in the south wall of the forecourt.

Contents page (left to right): South facade of the Big House (see also pp. 52–53); the Playhouse (see also pp. 94–95); the forecourt (see also pp. 136–137).

Editor: Jacqueline Decter
Designer: Patricia Fabricant
Production Editor: Owen Dugan
Production Manager: Lou Bilka

Additional Photography Credits
The National Trust for Historic Preservation, Pocantico Historic
   Area: pages 15, 21, 25
Courtesy of the Rockefeller Archive Center: pages 8, 10, 11, 12,
   13, 14, 16, 17, 18, 19, 20, 22, 23, 24, 26, 27, 28, 29, 30, 31,
   32, 33, 36, 38, 39, 40, 54, 55, 96, 97, 99, 100, 141, 142, 143,
   144, 145

First edition
10 9 8 7 6 5 4 3 2 1

*Library of Congress
Cataloging-in-Publication Data*
Roberts, Ann Rockefeller.
   The Rockefeller family home, Kykuit / photographs by
Mary Louise Pierson ; text by Ann Rockefeller Roberts ;
captions and additional text by Cynthia Altman.
         p.   cm.
   Includes index.
   ISBN 0-7892-0222-0
   1. John D. Rockefeller House (Pocantico Hills, N.Y.)
2. Eclecticism in architecture—New York (State)—Pocantico
Hills. 3. Pocantico Hills (N.Y.)—Buildings, structures, etc.
4. Delano & Aldrich. I. Altman, Cynthia. II. Title.
NA7238.P55R63   1998
728.8 '09747 '277—dc21
                                          97-39464

CONTENTS

Rockefeller Family Tree 6

Introduction 8

The Big House 52

The Outbuildings 94

The Gardens 136

Photographer's Note / Acknowledgments 188   Visitor's Guide / Bibliography 190   Index 191

THE ROCKEFELLER FAMILY TREE

THE BROTHERS AND ABBY | MARRIED

Abby Rockefeller (Babs)
1903–1976

David Milton• ········
Irving Pardee
Jean Mauzé

John Davison Rockefeller 3rd
1906–1978

Blanchette Ferry Hooker ········

THE FOUNDING FATHER

JOHN DAVISON ROCKEFELLER
1839–1937

~ married ~

Laura Celestia Spelman
1839–1915

THE SON

JOHN DAVISON ROCKEFELLER JR.
1874–1960

~ married ~

Abby Greene Aldrich ········
1874–1948

~ then married ~

Martha Baird Allen
1895–1971

NELSON ALDRICH ROCKEFELLER
1908–1979

Mary Todhunter Clark• ········
Margaretta Fitler Murphy ········

THE DAUGHTERS

Bessie Rockefeller
1866–1906

Alice Rockefeller
1869–1870

Alta Rockefeller
1871–1962

Edith Rockefeller
1872–1932

Laurance Spelman Rockefeller
b. 1910

Mary French ········

Winthrop Rockefeller
1912–1973

Barbara Sears• ········
Jeannette Edris•

David Rockefeller
b. 1915

Margaret McGrath ········

• Divorced

THE COUSINS	MARRIED	THE FIFTH GENERATION	
Abby Milton 1928	George O'Neill	George Dorr O'Neill Jr. 1950 Abby O'Neill 1953 David Milton O'Neill 1955	Catherine Mauzé O'Neill 1958 Wendy Harrison O'Neill 1962 Peter Meriwether O'Neill 1962
Marilyn Milton 1931–80	William Simpson	Laura Knickerbacker Simpson 1954 Abby Rockefeller Simpson 1958	
Sandra Ferry Rockefeller 1935		John Rockefeller 1969 Valerie Blanchette Rockefeller 1971	Charles Percy Rockefeller 1973 Justin Aldrich Rockefeller 1979
John Davison Rockefeller IV 1937	Sharon Percy		
Hope Aldrich Rockefeller 1938	John Spencer• Warren Kozak	David Hooker Spencer 1961 Benjamin Murray Spencer 1964 Theodore Spencer 1966	
Alida Davison Rockefeller 1949	Mark Dayton	Eric John Dayton 1980	Andrew Rockefeller Dayton 1983
Rodman Clark Rockefeller 1932	Barbara Olsen• Alexandra von Metzler	Meile Louise Rockefeller 1955 Peter Clark Rockefeller 1957	Stuart Alexander Rockefeller 1960 Michael Sorum Rockefeller 1964
Ann Clark Rockefeller Roberts 1934	Robert Pierson• Lionel Coste• T. George Harris•	Clare Marie Pierson 1956 Joseph Anthony Pierson 1957	Mary Louise Pierson 1959 Rachel Ann Pierson 1960
Steven Clark Rockefeller 1936	Anne-Marie Rasmussen• Dori Selene Liles	Steven Clark Rockefeller Jr. 1960 Ingrid Rasmussen Rockefeller 1963 Laura Selene Rockefeller 1981	Jennifer Rasmussen Rockefeller 1964
Michael Clark Rockefeller 1938–61			
Mary Clark Rockefeller 1938	William Strawbridge• Thomas Morgan	Geoffrey Tod Strawbridge 1963 Michael Rockefeller Strawbridge 1965 Sabrina Vaux Strawbridge 1968	
Nelson Aldrich Rockefeller Jr. 1964 Mark Fitler Rockefeller 1967			
Laura Spelman Rockefeller 1936	James Case III• Richard Chasin	Peter Rockefeller Case 1961 Matthew Owen Case 1964 Jessica Case 1967	
Marion French Rockefeller 1938	Warren Weber	Rachel French Weber 1967	Elizabeth Parmly Weber 1970
Lucy Aldrich Rockefeller 1941	Charles Hamlin• Jeremy Waletzky•	Jacob Peter Waletzky 1971	Naomi French Waletzky 1976
Laurance Rockefeller 1944	Wendy Gordon	Wyatt Gordon Rockefeller 1985	
Winthrop Paul Rockefeller 1948	Deborah Sage• Lisenne Dudderar	Andrea Davidson Rockefeller 1972 Katherine Cluett Sage Rockefeller 1974 Winthrop Paul Rockefeller Jr. 1976	
David Rockefeller Jr. 1941	Sidney Roberts• Diana Newell-Rowan	Ariana Newell Rockefeller 1982	Camilla Rockefeller 1985
Abby Aldrich Rockefeller 1943	Carl Lindstrom•	Christopher Rockefeller Lindstrom 1980	
Neva Goodwin Rockefeller 1944	Walter Kaiser•	David Walter Kaiser 1969	Miranda Margaret Kaiser 1971
Margaret Dulany Rockefeller 1947	David Quattrone•	Michael Dulany Quattrone 1977	
Richard Gilder Rockefeller 1949	Nancy Anderson	Clayton Anderson Rockefeller 1978	Rebecca Anderson Rockefeller 1980
Eileen McGrath Rockefeller 1952	Paul Growald	Adam Rockefeller Growald 1985	

Four generations at Kykuit: JDR (center), Jr. (left), and Nelson, holding his eldest child, Rodman.

Both John D. Rockefeller (JDR) and John D. Rockefeller Jr. (Jr.) loved beautiful views and had an inherent sense of the land and its spirit, although they might never have expressed it in quite that way. The land they chose at Pocantico is a testament to this innate sensibility. Located on a wide sweep of the Hudson River known as the Tappan Zee, it was formed when ancient glaciers carved out a great rift and rounded the mountains into hills. These full, rolling hills stretch back from the river; morning mist drifts among them, storms bear down along the river with sudden speed and power, evenings can be still and sweet or brilliant with the riotous colors of the setting sun. Gazing at the uninterrupted vistas, one has a startling sense of how this land must have looked before the first European settlers arrived— miles of deciduous and evergreen forest, the river a ribbon of undulating silver cutting through it.

The character of the land is felt in the many elements that comprise it: the rock ledges that form a massive crust underneath, barely hidden in spots, rising up through the earth in others; the mantle of earth over the rock, deep and rich in many places, shallow in others, but always full of loose stones (used by early settlers to form miles of walls, and reused by JDR and Jr. for house foundations, garden walls, and terraces); the wide variety of deciduous trees, including oak, elm, maple, butternut, walnut, and tulip; evergreens, such as pine, hemlock, and spruce; and myriad other native flora—dogwood, laurel, azalea, wildflowers, mosses, grasses, shrubbery, vines. The wildlife of the area was also originally very rich and varied; now it consists of creatures that can coexist more easily with humankind and that we are willing to tolerate in our midst: white-tailed deer with their large ears and bobbing tails, possums, raccoons, rabbits, mice, the occasional fox, hawks, owls, and a variety of songbirds, as well as the ubiquitous crow.

On this natural matrix the built elements were laid out and a great, parklike estate was developed. The land became highly cultivated in every sense of the word, reflecting the character and spirit first of the father and son and then of succeeding generations.

Each of the seasons is etched in color, form, and texture all around Pocantico. In the early spring the melting snow reveals the browns and grays of the sleeping land, and the architectural forms of the gardens and buildings stand out starkly. Then a pale green haze of tender new shoots and leaves sweeps over the trees and manicured lawns. Before long spring bulbs, shrubbery, and flowering trees all burst into bloom in the gardens. In the summer it is a tapestry of leaf textures and shades of green, the gurgle of water in fountains, the dappled patterns of sunlight through leaves, the music of wind through the trees, the purring of lawn mowers over the greensward of the golf course. In the fall color manifests itself again in the riotous turning of the leaves, in swaths of chrysanthemums, and in the last roses in the gardens. Then winter sets in, stripping everything of its last hues, returning the earth to browns and grays, and finally cloaking everything in the white of snow or the silver of ice, glittering in the pale sun on statues, garden walls, and plants.

The acquisition, development, and occupancy of Pocantico is intertwined with the lives of six generations of the Rockefeller family. It was intended to be—and always remained—a private home, the beloved country retreat of JDR and his wife, Laura Spelman Rockefeller, their children, and their children's children. The estate was developed between 1893, when JDR made the first purchase of land, and 1913, when the main house and its extensive gardens were largely completed. Since then there have been many more changes— additional land was acquired, other buildings were built, and each succeeding generation left its distinctive touch.

Until the last quarter of the nineteenth century JDR and his growing family lived exclusively in Cleveland, Ohio, where he developed the oil business that made him a wealthy and famous man. As the business expanded, however, he found himself spending more and more time in New York City. Eventually he began to bring his three daughters and young son, John Jr., with him on these extensive trips. By 1877 they were spending the entire winter in a New York hotel suite. But they still considered Cleveland home, and in 1878 JDR bought more than seven hundred acres of land at Forest Hill, just outside of Cleveland, which he gradually developed into a country retreat, where the family spent the summers. Inevitably, JDR's center of operations shifted to New York

City, and in 1884 he bought a furnished brownstone at 4 West Fifty-fourth Street. The family lived there from October to May, returning to Forest Hill for the summer.

In 1885 JDR's brother and business partner, William Rockefeller, bought a large estate on the Hudson River just north of Tarrytown. He spent $3 million transforming it into the most sumptuous estate in the area, complete with a huge Gothic stone house—Rockwood Hall—elaborate gardens, large stables, and liveried footmen at the door. William loved the Hudson River valley and began extolling the virtues and beauties of the area to his brother. JDR would spend summer weekends there when he could not join his family in Forest Hill and finally was persuaded to take a look around for himself.

In the summer of 1892 he and eighteen-year-old Jr. went to explore the land along the Pocantico, a stream that abutted his brother's property. In their characteristically meticulous fashion they first bought maps of the area and then walked all about until they came upon a hill rising some four hundred feet above the Hudson River to the west. Ascending to the top, they discovered that the views from it were magnificent. In the seventeenth century Dutch settlers had aptly named this hill Kykuit, meaning "high point" or "lookout." In earlier times it had apparently been used by the local Tappan Indians to survey the area or send signals. The highest hill in the region, it holds a commanding position along the ridge of land separating the Saw Mill River from the Hudson. There are clear views from it in all four directions, including west to the Hudson River just as it opens up wide into the Tappan Zee. In contrast to many of the other fine Hudson River valley estates, which are lined up one after the other right along the riverbank, the site is set back several miles from the river.

An early photograph of the Pocantico River; in the distance a wooden bridge spans the meandering stream.

It is no accident that JDR and Jr. set their sights on Kykuit Hill; JDR cared much more about views than about riverfront property. As he himself said: "At Pocantico Hills, New York, where I have spent portions of my time for many years in an old house where the fine views invite the soul and where we can live simply and quietly, I have spent many delightful hours, studying the beautiful views, the trees, and fine landscape effects of that very interesting section of the Hudson River, and this happened in the days when I seemed to need every minute for the absorbing demands of business." He inherited this independence of spirit and love of land from his father, a farmer, entrepreneur, and skilled horseman who insisted that the farms he bought be well situated and of graceful contour. This sensibility was also passed on to Jr., who as a young boy spent countless hours at Forest Hill watching his father lay out roads and move and plant trees.

After their explorations, JDR marked nine contiguous properties on the maps; the next summer he negotiated their price and bought them. These properties became the center of "Pocantico Hills Place," as JDR and Jr. first called it in their early letters to each other. Father and son then went about systematically acquiring additional land for what was to become their New York country home and eventually the family seat of their branch of the Rockefeller family. Sharing the vision of a family compound with Kykuit Hill at its center, they continued to expand their holdings over the next thirty years, until the property comprised more than three thousand acres. JDR worked quietly behind the scenes, using local real estate agents to buy properties for him so that he could be sure to get fair market prices. Neither father nor son felt it was necessary or proper to pay inflated rates, and they were willing to negotiate hard or bide their time to acquire a piece of land for the right price. The three hundred acres surrounding the Rockefellers' houses were eventually fenced in to keep the curious at bay and give the increasingly famous family some privacy. But the outer acreage, which includes farm buildings, fields for livestock and horses, and more than fifty miles of carriage roads, has always remained open, and the public has always had free access to the extensive trail system.

There were several houses already situated on the original parcels of land JDR purchased. Being extremely frugal, he bought these houses furnished whenever possible and used them for himself, his family, and his staff or rented them out while considering his options. He and Laura moved into one of these existing homes in the fall of 1893. The Parsons-Wentworth House, as it was known, with its stone coach barn and henhouse, was located on the northeast slopes of Kykuit Hill, just in front of the present Coach Barn. For eight years they contentedly spent winter weekends and part of each summer and fall in this house, sharing its upstairs rooms with their adult children and in-laws.

As soon as JDR settled into the Parsons-Wentworth House, he began to look for the optimal site for a new house. The top of Kykuit Hill had the finest views, but it was a rocky crag— wild, beautiful, and utterly unsuitable for building on. So he soon started to make plans for leveling the hilltop. Previous owners had erected a three-story observation tower on the hill that he contrived to move to a higher location, from which he could overlook all the surrounding land. He strengthened this tower with an iron frame and added an observation deck at the top for himself and his family. At the recommendation of William Rockefeller and William's son Percy, he engaged Warren Manning of the landscape design firm Olmsted, Olmsted and Elliott to assist in leveling the hilltop and to prepare de-

As evening falls, the cows find their way from the fields through this tunnel near the farm barn in the early part of the century.

signs for the whole estate, including roads. These early plans called for a level site to accommodate a rectangular house measuring sixty by seventy-five feet. After careful calculations, made at JDR's insistence, of the angles of the sun at various times of year, it was determined that the house would be oriented lengthwise on an ESE–WNW axis, so that it would reap maximum benefit from the best light the seasons had to offer. The approach to the house was to be from the northeast; the road would then pass in front of the house and exit to the southwest. The rest of the roads on the growing estate were planned as graceful, gently curving lines that would be hidden from view by being set into the earth below grade level. As the excavations on the hilltop proceeded, JDR decided to save the dug-up rock and soil and incorporate them into the foundation and platform of the house. Thus the basic form of the estate was laid out, the size of the house determined, and the ground prepared to receive it. JDR supervised this work personally, even deciding which trees were to be cut down and which were to be moved to accommodate the work.

At this point an issue surfaced that was to challenge JDR, his son, and everyone who worked on the design and implementation of Pocantico, and that issue was money. JDR had more than enough money to do whatever he wanted and then some, as his brother had done at Rockwood Hall. However, he and William had been raised on a farm where money was sometimes available and sometimes scarce, depending on the fortunes of their itinerant father. As the elder son, John was recruited at a young age by his religious and anxious mother to assume many of the responsibilities of his often absent father. He was taught to conserve and carefully tend limited resources. The Protestant ethic according to which he was raised also taught that indulgence of any kind was sinful and that money itself was dangerous to the health of the soul. These principles of frugality and plain living, combined with his clear vision, genius for organization, and passion for detail, brought him great success in his business endeavors. And they stayed with him all his life. So even as his wealth was skyrocketing into the hundreds of millions of dollars in the 1880s and 1890s, he carefully watched and counted his expenditures on the estate as if times had not changed. He compared costs at Pocantico with those at Forest Hill, wanting every penny to count and to be sure he was getting his money's worth. He had difficulty understanding that the cost of labor in the East was higher than in the Midwest, and he resented the fees of professionals such as architects and designers, believing that he could do their job himself, just as he had done at Forest Hill. He also had an abhorrence of what he considered unnecessary frills, preferring simple and straightforward design. As he told one biographer, "I hate frills. Useful things, beautiful things, are admirable; but frills, affectations, mere pretenses of being something very fine, bore me very much."

The Parsons-Wentworth house, where JDR and Laura lived when at Pocantico until it was destroyed by fire in September 1902. The porte-cochere is an artist's rendering; it was never added to the house.

His son was brought up to believe in the same religious precepts and shared his father's concern that fair value be given for the amount paid, as well as a keen sense of the importance of detail in attaining the desired result. But Jr. was the only son of a self-made man, brought up with comforts, privileges, and a much broader education. Unlike his father, he never experienced scarcity. As a result, he had a very different view of what constituted indulgence or wasteful extravagance and a much greater comfort level about spending money. He also was well aware of the tendency for fees and prices to escalate when the word spread that the work was for the Rockefellers. He never hesitated to get in other bids and was a hard bargainer when he thought he was being dealt with unjustly. The disagreements over finances between father and son, as well as between them and the professionals hired to design and carry out the work, caused tension and debate throughout the project.

As the cost of the excavation work on Kykuit Hill mounted, JDR began to question the expense and felt that the work was not being done as efficiently as possible. He pushed to get more work out of the men by increasing the supervision on the job. He was also impatient to see results. As he put it, "People no longer young wish to get the effects they desire at once." These tactics generated ill will among the workers, and on September 14, 1895, a suspicious fire broke out in the Parsons-Wentworth coach barn, henhouse, and greenhouse. Though it was thought to have been arson, no culprit was ever apprehended and no direct connection ever made, but the damage had been done, the buildings destroyed.

Despite this loss JDR and Laura continued to spend some weekends and the fall season in the Parsons-Wentworth House. The excavations progressed, and topsoil was brought in to cover the platform created for the house, although JDR's ardor for a new house on the crag was considerably dampened by the fire and other major difficulties in his business and personal life.

As a result of the passage of the Interstate Commerce Act in 1887 and the Sherman Antitrust Act in 1910; the subsequent government suits to break up Standard Oil; and the publication of Ida M. Tarbell's book *The History of the Standard Oil Company* in 1904, JDR was the object of an enormously hostile press and public throughout the period when he was developing Pocantico. To add to the pressures, local Tarrytown officials raised the taxes on his expanding properties exorbitantly, thinking perhaps that the town ought to have some benefit from his wealth. He took them to court and won, only to have them levy the taxes again in defiance of the ruling. The only way he was able to make peace and gain a just reduction in the taxes was to construct a new school building for the town, something they had been lobbying for all along. Although he never complained about or reacted outwardly to all the assaults on his career and his person, they must have taken a great toll. During this time he suffered from nervous indigestion and contracted alopecia nervosa, a viral infection that causes loss of all body hair. His wife, Laura, was also in ill health at that time.

JDR gradually disengaged himself from his contract with Warren Manning, reducing his commission to a small annual consultation fee in 1895 and to an "on call" arrangement in 1896. Manning made one last attempt in June 1896 to reengage JDR by submitting a complete estate plan for his consideration, but nothing came of it, and his retainer was canceled in January 1897. Although elements of Manning's design for the grounds are evident today, JDR maintained control and claimed the credit. As he said in a book of reminiscences, "Others may be surprised at my claim to be an amateur landscape architect in a small way, and my family have been known to employ a great landscape man to make quite sure that I did not ruin the place. . . . I had the advantage of knowing every foot of the land. . . . In a few days I had worked out a plan so devised that the roads caught just the best views at just the angles where in driving

The observation tower on the western slope of Kykuit Hill, from which JDR could survey the surrounding land.

up the hill you came upon impressive outlooks, and at the ending was the final burst of river, hill, cloud and great sweep of country to crown the whole; and here I fixed my stakes to show where I suggested that the roads should run, and finally the exact place where the house should be."

In the summer of 1897 Jr. graduated from Brown University and in the fall began to work in his father's offices in New York City. For the next three years he endured a difficult and trying initiation into his father's business world. He also seriously courted and finally won the hand of Abby Aldrich, daughter of Senator Nelson Aldrich of Providence, Rhode Island. They were married on October 9, 1901, and spent part of their honeymoon at Pocantico, where they were insulated from the prying eyes of the curious and the press.

During these years Jr. joined his father in what was to become an ever-increasing involvement in the development of the estate. His first project was to build a new coach barn behind the Parsons-Wentworth House. Late in 1899 he engaged the services of York & Sawyer, a newly formed New York architectural firm, to design the building. It was to house not only the family's horses, carriages, and sleighs but also all the maintenance vehicles and work animals. There were to be rooms for stable workers and a boiler room for the estate. Work on the building began in the summer of 1900 and took two years to complete. The stone was quarried on estate land, and estate labor was used, as both JDR and Jr. preferred. The building design and program were complicated to start with, involving substantial excavation and grade changes, yet JDR and Jr. requested many design changes as construction proceeded, causing delays and large cost overruns. This scenario was to play itself out time and again: careful and lengthy planning by all parties and modest cost estimates would be foiled by constant changes of design and materials, resulting in many delays and actual costs tallying as much as twice the original estimates. This large, heavy stone-and-brick building, constructed to be more fireproof than its predecessor, was the first new structure erected on the estate. It loomed over the modest wooden Parsons-Wentworth House, and the startling contrast between the two was also a strong indication of the differences between Jr.'s and his father's ideas for the estate.

About the turn of the century JDR was introduced to the game of golf while staying at a hotel in New Jersey. He was immediately taken with the sport and subsequently engaged the services of Jones Willie Dunn, a prominent designer of golf courses, to lay out a twelve-hole course around Kykuit Hill. In 1902, just as the Coach Barn was being completed at Pocantico, he bought a defunct country club with its own golf course in Ocean County, New Jersey. There, as at Forest Hill and Pocantico, he acquired the property with an existing building on it. He then hired Dunham A. Wheeler (1861–1938) as architect and remodeled the building to his liking. Golf became a favorite pastime for him, and he played regularly up until a year before his death at age ninety-seven. At both Lakewood House, as the Ocean County estate was called, and Pocantico he could play in privacy with people of his own choosing, safe from the pestering of the curious, the press, and those he viewed as scheming for his money.

On September 17, 1902, fire struck again, this time inside the Parsons-Wentworth House. JDR and Laura were at Forest Hill; Jr. and Abby were in New York City. Fortunately, it was

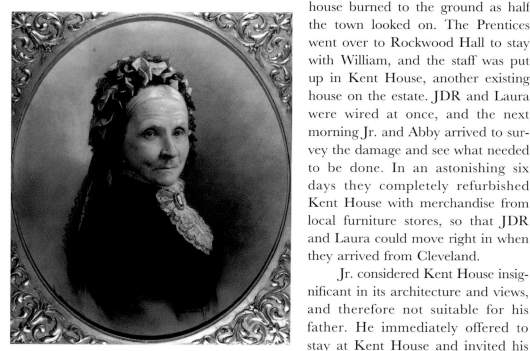

Portrait of JDR's mother, Eliza Davison Rockefeller, 1883, a pastel after a photograph by Sarony (probably Napoleon Sarony, 1821–1896). Jr. wrote on the back: "This hung in the dining room at Pocantico Hills during Father's life."

a slow electrical fire, allowing Jr.'s sister Alta, her husband, Parmalee Prentice, and the whole staff to escape without harm. They managed to drag some of the most important first-floor furnishings out onto the lawn. But everything in Jr. and Abby's rooms on the top floor directly above the fire was lost, including all of Jr.'s letters to Abby during their courtship. The fire trucks could do little to stop the fire, and the house burned to the ground as half the town looked on. The Prentices went over to Rockwood Hall to stay with William, and the staff was put up in Kent House, another existing house on the estate. JDR and Laura were wired at once, and the next morning Jr. and Abby arrived to survey the damage and see what needed to be done. In an astonishing six days they completely refurbished Kent House with merchandise from local furniture stores, so that JDR and Laura could move right in when they arrived from Cleveland.

Jr. considered Kent House insignificant in its architecture and views, and therefore not suitable for his father. He immediately offered to stay at Kent House and invited his parents to move into Abeyton Lodge, the house that JDR had bought and given to him and Abby as a wedding present in 1901. It had just been renovated and seemed to Jr. a much more fitting place. But JDR was perfectly content with the modesty of Kent House and settled in quite happily, looking forward to tinkering with it at his leisure and under his own direction.

Destruction of the Parsons-Wentworth House prompted both father and son to reconsider building a house on Kykuit Hill. Soon after the fire JDR asked Dunham A. Wheeler, who was already doing the renovations at Lakewood House, to draw up plans for a house. Jr. considered Wheeler's penchant for the Gothic Revival and half-timbered or shingled Queen Anne styles much too old-fashioned. It was of the utmost importance to him that his father's house be of a style that would do honor and justice to JDR's stature and accomplishments. In the fashion of the times, that meant a house designed in the Beaux Arts style. With this in mind, and without consulting his father, Jr. contacted Chester H. Aldrich (1871–1940), a distant cousin of Abby's. Aldrich and his partner, William A. Delano (1874–1960), were just establishing themselves in New York social circles as talented proponents of all things current and classical in architectural design. In a letter of October 24, 1902, Jr. told Aldrich that he had "a little business matter" to discuss, "the question of plans for my father's house at Pocantico Hills." He cautioned Aldrich that nothing might come of the matter, but after they met, Jr. commissioned Delano & Aldrich to draw up preliminary plans for a house on Kykuit Hill. Armed with these plans, Jr. went to his father to try to persuade him of the greater merits of his choice of architects. Thus began a discussion between the two men that would last for nearly four years until Jr. finally prevailed, Delano & Aldrich were hired, and construction on the house actually commenced. Discussions of this kind about every aspect of planning and construction continued as the house and grounds were developed, changed, and expanded over the years.

Although JDR stated repeatedly that all he wanted was a simple house in the country to share with his family, Jr. persisted, gently but doggedly, with his much grander plans. The correspondence between the two men on the subject is a fas-cinating record of how Jr. succeeded in building the house and gardens he envisioned for his father by professing his devotion to his father's wishes while persuading him of the validity of each step of this larger vision.

On September 7, 1907, for instance, Jr. wrote to JDR in defense of the continually escalating expenses for the gardens that William Welles Bosworth was designing: "When the gardens are completed I feel that you will be perfectly satisfied with them and that you will not regard the cost as excessive or unjustified. . . . Everyone who has seen the plan says that there is nothing comparable to it in this country. . . . But the difficulty is to satisfy you of these things in advance, particularly when there is at present apparently so little to show for the expenditure incurred to date. It has been my constant effort to keep the cost down to the lowest possible point and at the same time to do as perfect and lasting and satisfactory a piece of work as possible. . . . So enthusiastic am I about the gardens, so confident that you will take great pride and pleasure in them when completed, that I would be only too glad to pay one-half of the total cost of the finished gardens if you would permit, and it would give me as much pleasure to do this as it has to seek, all through the construction of the house and gardens, to bring about a result which I felt would meet with your approbation. I make this suggestion in all sincerity and earnestness and nothing would give me greater or more real satisfaction than to have you accept it."

JDR did not answer this letter until January 3, 1908. His reply was brief and did not respond at all to Jr.'s offer to

The wedding portrait of Abby Aldrich Rockefeller, Davis & Sanford, October 1901.

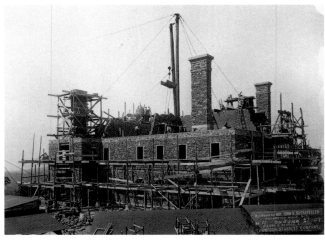

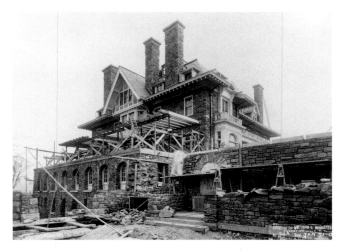

share in the cost. He directed his frustration at the contractors rather than at his son: "In regard to going forward with the construction of the garden, I think you better go forward . . . watching more closely than ever the cost, as it is evident to me that the contractors are in for just as much of the ten per cent business as they can introduce, even though it does unfairly tax us. It is not to be expected that we will receive fair treatment from the labor union forces."

Later that year, as it became more and more clear that the total cost of both the house and the gardens would be more than double the original modest estimates, JDR made more anxious inquiries of Jr., although in a letter dated September 23 he acknowledged the extent of Jr.'s efforts: "From all accounts I hear and from what I saw and knew of your faithful and intelligent devotion to this undertaking on behalf of your parents, coupled with the earnest, hearty and invaluable service of your beloved wife, I am sure we will all be satisfied."

Some time later Jr. wrote to his father, "I have felt throughout that in view of the immense amount of money you are constantly giving away to others and in view of the infinitesimal amount that you have spent for your own pleasure and enjoyment in your life, it was not inappropriate that you should have for yourself and for mother a place which would give you all the pleasure and enjoyment which could possibly be secured. I have probably been more generous in supplying things which I thought were conducive to that end than you yourself would have been."

JDR prevailed on certain basic issues, such as the size of the floor plan of the house and the relatively modest size of the rooms, but Jr. had his way in the end with the architecture and interior design; thus the overall scheme of the house and gardens met with his satisfaction.

Not surprisingly, JDR's greatest difficulty with the project lay in accepting the escalation in costs as construction progressed. Jr.'s original estimate for the house and gardens was about $500,000—a not inconsiderable sum in those days, but within reason to JDR's way of thinking. The actual cost, however, exceeded $1 million. This was very disturbing to him, not because they could not afford it or because Kykuit was any more expensive than the other great estates being built along the Hudson (in fact, it cost considerably less than most), but because JDR found it uncomfortable to spend large sums of money on himself. He lived a kind of contradiction in this regard; on the one hand he acquired and enjoyed several quite grand places, while on the other he lived in them in a very simple way and wrote frequently about the virtues of the simple life. "I am convinced," he once told a biographer, "that we want to study more and more not to enslave ourselves to things and get down more nearly to the Benjamin Franklin idea of living and take our bowl of porridge on a table without any tablecloth." It was as if his wealth and lifestyle had gotten way ahead of the beliefs he had acquired in his childhood.

Except for his constant grumbling and suspicions about the cost, JDR was happy to leave the architectural decisions to Jr., who went ahead and gave the job of designing the house to Delano & Aldrich. He also hired William Welles Bosworth to design and build the gardens. Every detail of the work was monitored by Jr., and it was clearly his vision, not his father's, that predominated in the end.

By 1908 the house was finished. Jr. and Abby scrupulously checked everything to make sure that all was in order and nothing had been left undone. They even slept in each of the bedrooms. Then they hovered anxiously as JDR and Laura finally moved in just in time for Thanksgiving.

Problems surfaced almost at once. Laura felt that the third-floor bedrooms under the steeply pitched roof were far too small to receive guests properly. The service entrance was situated directly under the master bedroom window, and the racket of delivery vehicles coming and going disturbed JDR and Laura's rest. The elevator and the water closets were noisy, too, and the house had several leaks. Perhaps the most troublesome flaw was the improper functioning of the down drafts in the chimneys, which brought smoke into many of the rooms, causing great discomfort as well as damage to the walls and furniture. JDR described the extent of the problem to Jr. in a letter: "I have been reviewing the experience with the chimneys since our last conversation on the subject. I had smoke of a few minutes only on lighting the fire in my bathroom. . . . We had smoke in the dining room, [even] on

Above: The gardens in August 1907 (top) and March 1908, as the stone walls begin to shape the landscape around the house.

Opposite: Photographs of the house taken by the construction company, Thompson-Starrett, March, June, and September 1907, as it rises from basement to roof.

standing the wood up to reduce the fire within the last three or four days. Auntie had bad smoke . . . in her room from a fire in the fireplace, and there was smoke in the room above it. . . . In the Drawing room, we had slight smoke within a week or ten days, without any fire, attributed to the down draught." This malfunction particularly irked JDR. In his youth he had designed and built a house for his parents in which they lived comfortably for some time, so he was, in his own words, "amazed all the time at the ignorance or negligence architects exhibit in carrying out practical work."

There was no question that these flaws had to be corrected. JDR had quite a few ideas of his own about how to remedy some of them. For instance, he conceived of a scheme to construct a service tunnel beneath the approach road so that deliveries would not be visible or within earshot of family or guests, and he proposed to Jr. that they consider raising the roof of the house in order to fix the faulty chimney drafts. "So desirous am I to have the chimneys right beyond per-adventure," he wrote, "that if it were not such tremendous trouble, I would be willing to run the walls of the house up higher, so that the main chimney could extend to the top of the roof." Jr. took these ideas to Delano & Aldrich, and in spite of the considerable additional expense, both of JDR's solutions were implemented. An elaborate tunnel leading to the service entrance was constructed. The roof was raised up and flattened out, the chimneys extended, and a fourth floor was added for staff, thereby creating a full third floor for guests.

All of these changes necessitated an entirely new design for the facade of the house. The original porch had to be re-

The original design of the west facade of Kykuit, spring of 1909 or 1910. To the right is the lattice arbor that once extended along the western terrace.

moved, and the interior of the house was going to become substantially larger. Jr. had developed a strong friendship with William Welles Bosworth while he was designing the gardens around the house, and over the strenuous objections of Delano and Aldrich, Jr. commissioned Bosworth to design the new facade and asked that all three architects work together on the reconstruction of the house. Delano and Aldrich could only swallow their professional pride and make the best of a most trying situation.

Bosworth further recommended to Jr. that the forecourt be redesigned and expanded so that it would properly complement the new and much grander Beaux Arts–style facade of the house. Jr. was persuaded, and after some initial resistance JDR himself became interested in the complex logistics of this project, which involved moving massive amounts of earth and constructing an intricate series of support arches under the platform holding up the forecourt. Obviously, JDR and Laura could not live in the house during such major alterations, so they moved back into Kent House for three years while the changes were being made. All the work, including the new forecourt, was finally completed in 1913, and JDR and Laura moved in again. This time all was well, and they settled into their new and greatly expanded home.

JDR and Laura enjoyed the comforts and beauty of Kykuit and its gardens together for two years. But in the spring of 1915, after struggling with poor health for many years, Laura died, leaving JDR alone in the huge house. From all reports, however, he continued to derive great pleasure from Kykuit after her death. He filled the house with many guests from his business, philanthropic, and religious circles and surrounded himself with family. He invited a distant cousin, Mrs. Fannie A. Evans (1862–1944), to come live with him as house manager and companion. He also had a devoted Swiss valet, Mr. Yordi, who was with him until his death. Moreover, Kykuit was not nearly as impersonal in style or scale as many mansions of that period because of JDR's early insistence on keeping the proportions of the individual rooms homey rather than palatial. Kykuit was first and foremost a home, not a showplace, and everything about its appointments bespoke comfort.

JDR's favorite activity at Kykuit was his daily round of golf. He was always accompanied by a family member or obliging guests and a young caddy from town. His grandsons or their wives were often conscripted into service. One of the wives remembers her first such outing, soon after she was married, with wry humor. JDR placed himself firmly in front of the ball to tee off, hands trembling, golf club wobbling, looking up and down unsteadily. She was sure he could not possibly hit the ball, but finally he swung, hitting the ball squarely and sending it a fair distance. Then it was her turn. She had played only a few times, and in spite of her youth, her steady hand, and her clear eye she could only dig a hole in the tee, missing the ball altogether on that first try. She also observed that part of the caddy's job was to run ahead and make sure JDR's ball was favorably placed for his next shot, a service the guests did not receive. For a man in his nineties who took such pleasure in the game, this seemed a fair arrangement.

His first great-grandchild, Abby Milton O'Neill, remembers being taken down with her baby sister to meet her great-grandfather on the second tee. She was no more than four, with long curls and all dressed up in a ruffled dress. She was given a club and invited to take a swing at the ball. "The only time I hit it," she says, "was when I dropped the club to run away and it hit the ball off the tee."

If JDR's hand was unsteady as he passed into his eighties and nineties, his mind was not. He retained a great interest in business events and kept a ticker tape wherever he was so that he could monitor the stock market. According to several of his grandsons, he traded considerable amounts and was very adept at it. During the stock market crash of 1929 he apparently bought a huge number of shares in Standard Oil to show his support for the company and to indicate his confidence that business in America was fundamentally healthy and would recover.

Jr., Abby, and their children lived right down the hill in Abeyton Lodge, and there were frequent visits back and forth. Sunday lunches became an institution, with all the children trooping up the hill to Kykuit to visit their grandfather and play in the gardens and fountains around the

A view of the east facade of Kykuit as it was redesigned by William Welles Bosworth in 1913, and as it is today.

house after lunch. JDR presided at the head of the table, and there were frequently other guests as well, including Baptist ministers, missionaries, and business acquaintances. Sometimes the aeolian organ in the music room would be played by Virgil Fox, the organist at Riverside Church in New York, or the player organ would be turned on. JDR often told his grandchildren stories with a little moral at the end or played games with them, such as Numerica, a popular number game, and he had a store of jokes that he told over and over when he had an audience. His grandchildren and some of his great-grandchildren remember him as a genial and devoted elder who took genuine pleasure in seeing them. As his youngest grandson, David Rockefeller, said, "He was an old man, very happy within his own skin" and therefore able to take pleasure in his family and in all he did.

He had a special relationship with David, who visited him often. Sometimes they had breakfast together, and JDR would explain the importance of chewing food thoroughly—up to twenty-seven times per bite, even if the food was milk! One memorable evening young David cooked a chicken dinner for JDR and Mrs. Evans at the Playhouse. He says he was no more than eleven or twelve at the time and that to his delight JDR pronounced the meal quite delicious.

David's brother Laurance also recalls his grandfather with great admiration. As a young person he was especially taken with JDR's philosophy of life, and he remembers a little rhyme JDR used to recite that in its simplicity said a great deal:

I was early taught to work as well as play;
My life has been one long, happy holiday,
Full of work and full of play,
I dropped the worry by the way
And God was good to me every day.

Top: Laurance, Babs, Nelson, and John 3rd riding in a wicker governess's cart, 1911. Above: Abby and Jr.'s children in 1917 (left to right): Babs, John 3rd, Nelson, Laurance, Winthrop, and David.

He was amazed by how detached JDR was from the great fortune he had established, as well as by how he was able to retire before his sixtieth year without a backward glance and eventually relinquish his extensive philanthropic endeavors. He saw how utterly comfortable he was with his life and his work, keeping his own counsel and choosing not to embroil himself in the controversies swirling around the Standard Oil Company. He admired JDR's decision to spend the end of his life with family and friends, and pursue his favorite personal activities in such contentment and peace.

The celebration of JDR's birthday was another regular family event. Everyone who was around gathered at Kykuit to dine. In fact, Jr. and Abby's annual trip to Maine was always scheduled for July 9, the day after JDR's birthday party. Abby described one of these gatherings in a letter to her son JDR 3rd: "I know you will be interested to hear about the Birthday Party which was a great success. . . . The morning of the birthday, as usual, was devoted chiefly to having photographs taken. This time we had a new photographer, and he took the pictures out in the garden. I think they are going to be very lovely. Your grandfather was taken practically with everyone, and we had family groups and the children alone and the children with their parents and in every possible combination, Nelson engineering the whole thing. . . . There were about twenty four at the birthday dinner. . . . Mr. Gibson played the organ during the dinner and afterwards we had the chief tenor from Radio Center sing for us. It was a perfectly heavenly night and we sat out on the Piazza while he sang lovely things like 'Oh Moon of my Delight,' 'Silvia,' 'Goodnight Sweetheart,' and some Italian songs. He sang beautifully and Mr. Gibson was a perfect accompanist. . . . After the music was over Nelson and Mary and Papa and I wandered about the gardens which were all lighted."

David remembers these celebrations well, especially JDR's eightieth birthday, when he gave five-dollar gold pieces to everyone present. David was five years old at the time and has his gold piece to this day.

In the afternoons JDR often went for drives in his roadster, taking guests or family with him for company. He would survey the grounds, deriving enormous pleasure from the beauty of the place he and his son had cultivated with such care. Well into his eighties he continued his landscaping interests, checking on trees to be moved or planted and making notes of landscaping changes he was thinking about.

JDR at Kykuit, 1930. This photograph was used as a Christmas card.

On May 23, 1937, in his ninety-seventh year, JDR died peacefully at his winter home in Ormond Beach, Florida. The funeral was held in New York, and he was buried in Cleveland next to his wife and mother. His death must have left a great void in the life of every member of the family. Not only was he the family patriarch and founder of their material wealth, but his spiritual beliefs and ethics were the basis of their values. Jr. was perhaps the most deeply affected. He was the only son, and a large part of his life had been devoted to attending to his father's interests. The two men had forged a unique and tightly woven relationship, born not only of circumstances but of mutual respect and deep affection. They had succeeded in working closely in all aspects of their lives despite very different personalities and styles of management. Kykuit was one result of their collaboration, and they had lived side by side on the estate for more than forty years.

Now Jr. was the sole heir and proprietor of Pocantico. One can only imagine how it must have felt to be living at last in the house that he had exerted so much effort to bring into being in spite of his father's misgivings and differences, the house that he and Abby had worked tirelessly to furnish and decorate in the best fashion of the times. Both Abby and Jr. loved Kykuit and lavished their attention and care on it. It became their weekend and part-time summer home for the rest of their lives.

They moved into Kykuit in the fall of 1937 and at once made plans to repaint the entire house and do some decorating. So in November of that year they returned to Abeyton Lodge for several months while the work was being done. In deference to JDR and Laura's memory they decided not to use the west-facing rooms on the second floor that had been theirs, choosing instead the east-facing rooms overlooking the entrance court. Abby turned one of the rooms into a lovely small sitting room and study for herself, choosing the furniture, colors, and paintings to create an inviting, cozy space filled with the morning sun. Jr. had his own study and dressing room overlooking the inner garden to the south. "We are all safely and peacefully moved into Mr. Rockefeller Sr.'s house," Abby wrote, "and everything seems to be running smoothly there. Really, it is a great pleasure to us all to be there. Apparently the children had never paid much attention to it, but since I have changed things around and made it more homelike, they all love it. . . . We are going to close the Lodge for the winter and will all spend our weekends at Kykuit."

As soon as they were settled in, they opened the doors to their family. Although their children were nearly grown by this time and most already married, they all had rooms they could call their own, and they came to spend weekends in this grand and beautiful place until they had country places of their own. Interestingly enough, Jr. seems to have had no objection to his children spending the night in his parents' rooms, even though he did not wish to do so himself. His oldest son, John (JDR 3rd), stayed there with his wife, Blanchette, as did some of the others. Nelson and his wife, Mary, and David also had rooms on the second floor, David's facing north overlooking the rose garden. Winthrop, Laurance and his wife, Mary, and Jr.'s daughter, Abby, and her husband, David Milton, had rooms on the third floor. None of them had grown up at Kykuit, of course. Abeyton Lodge just down the hill had been their childhood weekend home. David is the only one of his generation who had resided in the house for any length of time, having spent the fall and winter of 1938–39 at Kykuit writing his Ph.D. dissertation. He thought he would be able to work without distractions there, but it just so happened that Peggy McGrath lived nearby, and he had come to be very interested in her company. She came over often, and they courted on long horseback rides, picnics, and walks over the grounds. One evening at winter's end he proposed to her, and the next evening, after what must have been a very long twenty-four hours for the young suitor, she accepted his offer.

Jr. and Abby's firstborn was named Abby after her

A family portrait on the south porch of Kykuit, c. 1936, by Ira L. Hill. Left to right: Jr., Abby, Laurance, JDR, Winthrop, Abby (Babs) Rockefeller Milton, Nelson.

mother, but to distinguish between them they called her Babs. Babs had two daughters herself by this time, Abby and Marilyn. The third Abby was known as Mitzi when she was young. For several years, until they went off to boarding school, Mitzi and Marilyn often visited their grandparents on spring and fall weekends. Their mother did not particularly care for the country, so she sent the two of them to Kykuit with their nanny. They were given permanent bedrooms and a playroom on the fourth floor, overlooking the southern gardens. The two little girls were allowed to pick out the wallpaper themselves, from samples of French hand-painted, floral-patterned paper.

Mitzi recalls that some mornings they breakfasted with the housekeeper in the staff quarters down in the basement. Sometimes they were invited to sit with their grandmother in her bedroom; while she had breakfast on a tray, they would perch on the end of her bed, entranced by the delicate china, silver, and linen and by their grandmother in her ruffled bed jacket. Then they would run into their grandfather's study to chat with him while he ate his breakfast.

They learned that Jr. had a routine that he maintained every day, unless some business or personal event intervened. He rose early, and after breakfast his horse was brought to the front door for a morning ride. On these rides he often made tours of the estate, checking the progress of various projects, greeting the workers, giving instructions to the superintendent. He loved these rides and took much pleasure in surveying and tending to his property. He would return about ten o'clock and work until lunchtime. Wherever he was, his secretary was always by his side, ready to take letters and instructions. After lunch he worked again until midafternoon, when he would go for a carriage drive with Abby. The carriage would arrive at the front door, she would enter it from the high front step designed specially for that purpose, and off they would go, taking the two girls with them. The driver sat behind while Jr. drove, and the horses had tasseled net coverings on their ears to keep the flies away.

In the afternoons the two sisters sometimes had tea with their grandmother in her second-floor sitting room, while she reclined on the chaise longue. Abby spent a great deal of time in this room, resting, working on her many projects, and writing letters and postcards to her children and numerous grandchildren.

In the evenings an even greater treat awaited the girls. "Grandmother would have us come down and help her choose the dress and slippers that she would wear that evening to dinner," Mitzi remembers. After her bath she would emerge into the dressing room "in that long droopy underwear everybody wore then. Several things were put out and we would choose. There were great lessons in putting things together, and she would counsel us, saying, 'Those slippers don't look well with the dress, these would be better here, do you see that?' Then we would help her pick out the jewelry, going excitedly through the pieces she had put out, choosing between this and that. She would wear a long evening gown every evening, whether it was for guests or just for the two of them. It was a routine beyond belief."

JDR with his granddaughter, Abby (Babs) Rockefeller Milton, and her two daughters, Marilyn and Abby (Mitzi), on the south porch of Kykuit in the early 1930s.

After dinner the player organ was often turned on; if there were guests, Virgil Fox might play the aeolian organ, its rich sounds reverberating throughout the house. When they were at home by themselves, Jr. loved to read aloud to Abby, and many evenings were passed in this way. As far as guests

were concerned, Jr. and Abby continued the tradition started by JDR. The house was often full of friends from their religious, philanthropic, business, and artistic endeavors, including William Welles Bosworth; Raymond Fosdick, the lawyer and president of the Rockefeller Foundation from 1936 to 1948; his brother Harry Emerson Fosdick, the pastor of Riverside Church; Canadian prime minister McKenzie King; Baptist ministers; missionary doctors from China; and many other leaders and thinkers of the time. As the interests of Jr. and Abby were wider than JDR's, so was their circle of friends, and Kykuit continued to be a place where ideas were tried out, issues of the time addressed, and institutions incubated. It resembled a retreat, a place for people to think about and debate issues far from the pressures of daily life.

Sunday lunches at Kykuit evolved and grew as Jr. and Abby's six children started families of their own. Many of us in the fourth generation remember getting dressed up in our Sunday best, going off to church, and then on up to the "Big House," as we came to call Kykuit.

It was a very particular and predictable family rite. "We were given strict instructions about dining room behavior by our parents and our nannies," recalls David Rockefeller Jr. "We knew it was a formal occasion, and if we arrived at five to one we used to drive around the [entrance] circle until it was one o'clock. Grandfather did not like people to be early, and he definitely did not like people to be late. It was good to be sort of hovering in the holding zone like an airplane waiting to land. Then we would pull up at exactly one o'clock and he would greet us at the door." The format never varied, although the details were different enough to be intriguing to a child. After the formal greetings everyone would walk into the living room, where the children were expected to sit quietly and talk only if spoken to until lunch was served. "We were all just trying our hardest to be very good, and Grandfather would ask us how we were doing. Finally, lunch would be announced. William the wonder butler would open the double pocket doors and we would be invited in. And that clear soup in the lacquered bowls would be on the table. The bowls were covered with a top that looked like a bottom. After we were seated, the tops would be removed, and steam would come up." The menu had its own predictability and variations: would there be roast beef or turkey, homemade ice cream with fruit of the season or cottage pudding? Would the pudding have blueberry or butterscotch sauce? The thick whipped cream from Grandfather's cows was always there to top it off. What kind of flowers would Grandmother have put in the finger bowls—scented geranium leaves, pansies, or another seasonal blossom?

Grandfather always sat at one end of the table and Grandmother at the other. He had his own kind of dry wit, and sometimes he told us jokes. "Almost every time," a cousin remembers, "he told the one about the peas, the honey, and the knife. 'I eat my peas with honey, I've done it all my life. Although it may seem funny, it keeps them on the knife.' If he didn't tell it, we would always ask him to. I suppose we asked because it was about bad table manners when we were trying so hard to have good manners, and the story and the laughter were a sort of relief."

After lunch we returned to the living room, where the grown-ups were served coffee in delicate demitasse cups, and we again were to sit quietly, waiting. Would grandfather read to us from *Tom Brown's School Days,* or would we play Authors? Would we get to go upstairs to explore the seemingly infinite

Abby and her three eldest grandchildren (left to right): Marilyn and Abby (Mitzi) Milton, and Rodman Rockefeller.

number of rooms and drawers, or would we go outside and run through the gardens, playing hide-and-seek in the myriad nooks and crannies? The house was filled with family photographs of august ancestors and of our parents as small children, wonderful and beautiful objects from foreign countries, and white leather-bound books of fairy tales illustrated by Arthur Rackham. Everything seemed perfect and had an almost magical order and beauty. It was both soothing and intimidating. And as fascinating as it was to visit, it was hard to imagine living in this amazing house.

Nelson's eldest son, Rodman, remembers being taken upstairs to a second-floor guest room for a nap. "It was broad daylight, and at ten years old, you don't feel like resting. What do you do? I had a little Boy Scout screwdriver. I got a little restless and took Grandmother's clock down off the mantel and took it apart. Needless to say, when it came time to put it back together again, I was unable to do so. There were little pieces scattered all across the bed. You can imagine what happened. I'm sure they had to pick up all the pieces and ship them to the clockmaker."

During these lunches we became well acquainted with the very differing characters of our grandparents. "Most of us saw Grandfather as a pretty imposing figure who liked things to be just so," David Jr. says, "and yet there was a gentle aspect to him and a concerned aspect, too. Grandmother was a woman with so much warmth who enjoyed the physical, rather unruly presence of young children in a way that Grandfather never did." "He was a fairly self-contained and strict figure," says another cousin. "She was a loving, maternal, big-bosomed woman who enfolded you in her arms. I remember talking to her during World War II about her sons who were scattered around the world and her genuine concern for them. She would tell us what they were doing from their letters." And she also kept track of their battalion mates, sending some of them notes or hand-knitted gifts if they did not have family to write to.

Grandfather had a small, very elegant folding ruler that he carried with him everywhere and was clearly very attached to. Sometimes he let one of us look at it, unfold it, and measure things. On one of these occasions it got broken. It was a bad moment, resulting in "a frigid atmosphere of disapproval and icy stares from Grandfather. It was worse than if he had spoken angrily," Rodman recalls.

The lunches were sometimes full of surprises. One of Jr. and Abby's sons brought home to meet the family a number of the eligible young women he was seeing, including Broadway star Mary Martin. Aunt Lucy Aldrich, Abby's independent and outspoken sister, who was quite hard of hearing, often came to stay and would of course be at Sunday lunch. "She always sat on Grandfather's right," Mitzi recalls, "and I remember just as he lowered his head, she would pretend that she was deaf as a stone, and she would ask outrageous questions right as he started to say grace. It didn't happen once in a while, it happened quite frequently." Jr. would patiently put his hand on her arm, quietly lean over, and say, "Lucy, we are saying grace now."

Abby loved to have tea in the gardens or on the terrace with her daughters-in-law and grandchildren, selecting different places at different times of year or according to her mood. One of her favorite spots was her rose garden, where she took tea in the dappled shade of an arbor and could look out over the Hudson or at the flowers themselves—a study in shades of pink, red, yellow, and white. Sometimes she preferred one

Abby and Jr. taking a drive in an open carriage. Carriage driving is a tradition that continues to this day on Pocantico's fifty-five miles of carriage roads and trails.

of the arbors that looked down on the three interconnected stone pools under the elms. There she could delight in the light playing in softly moving patterns on the grass and water. She also loved the morning garden behind the teahouse, where she could sit and watch her grandchildren splash about in the little round pool. The possibilities were endless, and she enjoyed each outing to the fullest.

Both Abby and Jr. were as open to having their grandchildren visit the Big House as JDR had been, and for many of us in the fourth generation the estate was a place of great freedom, where we could safely roam at will, explore, build little clubhouses, play fantasy games, and experience the natural world. Like most of our uncles, many of us took our first swim in the shallow round pool in the morning garden with our grandmother Abby or nannies or mothers sitting close by. As we got older we would play in all the fountains—jumping into one, splashing about, dancing in the cascading water, and then running on to the next.

Thinking back, many of us recall the beauty of the grounds, "the smell of fresh-cut grass, the coming and going of Canada geese." Others mention the sound of the huge lawn mowers on hot summer mornings, the wind in the white pines out the window, "hearing the Coach Barn clock ring out the hours against the absolute stillness of the black country night," and "the gentle splashing sound of the many fountains in those beautiful gardens." "There was a wonderful feeling of being part of this great sculptured landscape," says David Jr. "I think that the beauty of the place just communicated itself to us. Even though we were just 'playing,' we were soaking in the wonder of this place at the same time."

Two of our cousins spent many early mornings as

adolescents riding their ponies, Queenie and Prince, over the lawns with wild abandon. "We rode over the sand pits in the golf course, and we rode over the greens, and we rode over everything we could think of riding over." At night they would ride "bareback under the moon over the golf course, feeling a part of our horses as we galloped up and down over the hills, thoroughly convinced that we knew the secret joy of being Indians." Once they camped out under the blue spruce trees near the Japanese pond, "waking to see an enormous red moon rise in the dark sky." Thinking it was on fire, they ran to wake one of their parents.

Most of us were taught to ride by Joe Plick, a wonderful wiry man and an excellent horseman who had spent some time as a trick rider in the circus. We first learned to ride on Rastus, a very amiable retired circus pony, among others. Then we practiced in the ring outside the stables, learning to trot and canter, change gaits, and manage our mounts. Finally we were allowed to go out on the trails on the thoroughbreds. "We would ride out of that huge stable, our horses' shoes echoing on the stone floor and the enormous glass globes hanging down. We would go for long rides with Joe," Rodman recalls. Some of the horses were named after us by Grandfather. Riding our namesakes was not necessarily an advantage, because they tended to be fiery and willful—quite a handful for young, inexperienced riders to control. Joe also organized horse shows, which our parents, grandmother, and grandfather dutifully attended, Grandmother always bedecked in one of her large, flowery hats. She described one of these shows in a letter to Winthrop: "It was a most extraordinary sight. All the grandchildren were there with the exception of the two tiny babies, which meant 15 chil-

dren milling about. All of them seemed perfectly happy and independent, paying very little attention to any of the grownups. Joe had appointed your father [Jr.] and Blanchette as judges. Blanchette made all the ribbons . . . it must have taken her hours . . . they had three awards, first prize blue ribbon, second red, and third yellow, and as there were just exactly three children in each class, everybody got a ribbon. I have a suspicion that there was a little question as to the impartiality of the judges, but they all took it extremely well, and those who didn't get a blue said they would next year and asked me why I wasn't a judge. I told them I thought Joe didn't ask me because he knew I would insist on blue ribbons for all of them. The show lasted three hours and ended when everyone gathered around Joe and gave him three lusty cheers."

Joe would conclude each show by driving a four-in-hand while standing atop his horse. He decided that we, too, could learn to ride standing up on the horse's back. He would attach a wide leather strap to our waist. A long rope connected the strap to a pole in the center of the ring. We then had to stand up on the backs of our ponies and go around the ring. If we lost our balance, we would go flying through the air like little fish on the end of a line! Not too many of us took to this stunt for long, and none of us chose circus riding as a career, but we loved the excitement and daring of it all the same.

The Coach Barn was a favorite place for those of us who loved riding and lived on the estate or close by. "My association with the stable was stronger than my association with the top of the hill. It was more fun, I felt freer there," says one cousin. "Kykuit was a distant historical site to me, not something I felt intimacy or involvement with." We would unsaddle

The path parallel to Kykuit's north facade and the pergola of the rose garden (one of Abby's favorite spots), by landscape photographer Mattie Edwards Hewitt, 1920s.

and groom our horses, care for the tack, and then climb up the circular metal staircase to visit Joe and his wife, Julia, who lived on the second floor. Julia Plick would offer us delicious cookies or cake while Joe regaled us with stories of his circus days.

The stables occupied half of the main floor of the Coach Barn; in the other were the cars, another source of fascination. There were JDR's old roadster, our parents' cars, and the electric car that Grandmother and Grandfather used for driving around the estate. "It was silent, so we never heard them coming," a cousin recalls. "All we would hear were the wheels crunching on the gravel driveway just as they arrived. They would come coasting up to the front of the house, have a little chat with us, and off they would go again. That was a humanizing element." We would climb in and out of all these vehicles, pretending to be important grown-ups. Best of all, there was a marvelous little two-seater roadster known as the Crosley Hotshot, in which we all learned to drive as we came of age. First we practiced out on the lawns with our fathers, jolting and lurching along until we got the hang of the gears, clutch, and brakes. Then we were let loose on the estate roads, and as our

The swimming pool terrace with grotto and "graceful little summer houses with round windows recalling Chinese design," Mattie Edwards Hewitt, 1920s.

confidence mounted we'd career down them at what we thought were breakneck speeds. Luckily for all, the car had a speed control on it, so our enthusiasm had built-in limits. Our uncles and aunt had learned to drive in this way as well; their training car was a small four-wheel buckboard with a maximum speed of 25 miles per hour.

To some the Coach Barn was overbearing. As David Jr. remembers, "Everything was so big in there where the cars are. There was grandeur, excitement, but something almost a little sinister. The stones were so big, the ceilings very high,

and the sound in there felt quite antihuman. As a small person it was a relief to have that little door" set into the giant double entry door. "It was on more of a human scale."

As much freedom as there was within the protective walls of the estate, there were restraints as well. Jr. was very particular about where we built our little clubhouses. If they interfered with his precious views in the slightest, one cousin remembers, "Grandfather would come and say, 'Well, you can't build it here, you can't have it there, because we will see it, we will see it in that place, so you have to take it away.'" Those of us whose parents had homes on the estate grounds always felt we were being checked up on and monitored—at times when we least suspected it—to make sure that we did not disrupt the studied perfection of the lawns, gardens, and shrubbery.

The same walls built to ensure privacy and protection also closed out the rest of the world, and some cousins keenly felt the isolation. "A verdant cage" is how one cousin describes it, remembering the loneliness she and others experienced. Friends and neighbors could not just come over to play without all kinds of special arrangements being made. There were gates and guards and, after the Lindbergh baby kidnapping, guard dogs as well. To us as small children it was a "riddle why [the walls] were there and why the guards were there, and why the dogs were there. What did that mean about who was outside the gates? Who was out there?"

The grounds and buildings were so grand that we feared that our friends would feel awestruck or envious. We felt separate, different, not sure whether our friends wanted to see us or visit the estate. After they saw the place, we wondered whether they still cared about us or were just using us as the means to this luxurious end. One cousin remembers her birthday party at the wonderful Playhouse; her whole class was invited despite her misgivings and protestations, and she felt extraneous to the whole affair. To her it was as though the party was for their entertainment and had little to do with celebrating her birth or her person.

We often made friends with the staff and grounds workers, searching for some direct connection to the ordinary daily lives of others. Many of those friendships were wonderfully nourishing and rewarding, providing balance, teachings about life, and companionship. One such person was Tom Pyle, manager of the woodlands and wildlife both inside and outside the gates of the estate. He was always available to talk with us about the natural world and take us with him on patrol, showing us new fox kits or a nest of baby rabbits. Two others were Nora and Henry Cotton. Their domain was the Playhouse, and they not only kept it spotless—the floors shining from Henry's rigorous polishing—but always had time to listen to our chatter and concerns while fixing us lunch or to tell us a story about their home in the South. Henry even found time to teach us to bowl and watched over our antics in the gym and the pool.

As the fourth generation matured during the turbulent 1960s, it became increasingly difficult for us to reconcile the luxury and physical beauty of Pocantico with the suffering and angry clamoring for change of our contemporaries. So we left, determined to find our own ways, succeed at our own professions, create our own families, and try to make peace with the wealth we had inherited. But there was always a thread of

attachment tugging at us. As Abby O'Neill puts it, "Whether we like it or not, it is a place that we identify with. For some it is more painful than for others. For [some] it is a pleasure, it just depends. Still, you know where you came from."

One of the threads that kept pulling us back was the impulse to gather together as cousins and in-laws. JDR and Jr. met for business and pleasure all their lives, Jr.'s daughter and five sons congregated for the same reasons, so we continued the tradition. We were drawn together not only by common business and philanthropic interests and obligations but also by the desire to understand who we were and what it meant to be a Rockefeller, to support one another in our pursuits both in and out of our growing clan. Eventually, as more of us came to these gatherings and our agendas grew longer, the Playhouse became the logical place for us to meet. It provided ample space for both work and relaxation.

The Playhouse was built by Jr. between 1925 and 1927 on a rise just above Abeyton Lodge as a place of recreation for the whole family and their friends. Duncan Candler, the architect who had renovated Abeyton Lodge for Jr. and Abby in an English-Norman style in 1914, was asked to build the Playhouse in a compatible style. The interior included a swimming pool, a bowling alley, a pool room, and a gymnasium, as well as a two-story living room with baronial fireplaces and a card room. In 1938, the year after JDR died, an indoor tennis court was added. Jr.'s sons and daughter were adults by the time the Playhouse was completed, so they missed the joys its dazzling array of choices offered to children, but they soon began to use it for their own parties, gatherings with friends,

David and Winthrop Rockefeller on the trails with Fred Rowe, coachman and riding instructor from 1898 to 1940, in 1920.

and personal meetings. After Sunday lunch with their parents at Kykuit, all six of them would often go down to the Playhouse and sit in the living room discussing business, philanthropic, and personal matters.

In 1948 Abby Aldrich Rockefeller died at home in her sleep. Her departure was deeply mourned by Jr. as well as by her children and grandchildren. She had been his closest companion, guide, and beloved partner for almost fifty years. Her vitality, creativity, and joyous, generous nature had enlivened everything she did and everyone who came into contact with her. She had been an integral part of all that happened on the estate, watching over the gardens, the houses, and the staff. She stayed in close touch with her children, in-laws, and numerous grandchildren right up until her death, remembering all of their birthdays (not one would go by without a present from her) and writing a stream of friendly, newsy letters and postcards to all. Her achievements were not limited to her home and family, however. Among her remarkable accomplishments in the world at large was the founding of the Museum of Modern Art.

After Abby's death Jr. continued his visits to Kykuit in the spring and fall, filling the house with family and friends to assuage his loneliness, just as his father had. His oldest grandchildren often joined him on weekends. In 1951 he married Martha Baird Allen (1895–1971), a pianist and the widow of an old friend. She became his companion during his last years. As he grew increasingly frail he was forced to give up his lifelong love of riding and carriage driving. He did not relinquish his weekend drives through the estate, however; he and Martha would visit new landscaping projects or favorite picnic sites and drive along the carriage roads to take a look at his cherished views. His grandchildren remember him at Kykuit close to the end, sitting in a wheelchair, his body frail but his mind clear, happy to see his ever-growing family, including his first great-grandchildren, and on occasion agreeing to be photographed with them.

Christmas 1955. Top row, left to right: Steven Clark Rockefeller, Nelson, Robert L. Pierson; middle row: Mary Clark Rockefeller, Mary Todhunter Clark Rockefeller, Ann Rockefeller Pierson; bottom row: Michael Clark Rockefeller, David Rockefeller Jr.

Jr. died in 1960. His death marked the end of an era for his family and the estate. For the first time since it was built, Kykuit was empty. JDR 3rd, Nelson, Laurance, and David assumed ownership and management of the estate. Babs had made her home in Long Island years before, and Winthrop had chosen to live in Arkansas; both relinquished their interests in the family seat. JDR 3rd and David had built their own country homes near the estate on land given to them by Jr. Nelson and Laurance were the only ones who had houses on the grounds, and the honor of becoming the next resident of Kykuit was assumed by Nelson. He loved its grandeur, the beauty of the gardens, and the spectacular views just as his father and grandfather had, and he had always dreamed of living there.

By 1961 all arrangements had been made among the brothers for Nelson to move into Kykuit, and they had received the consent of Martha Rockefeller, Jr.'s widow. As his father and mother had done before him, he immediately started making plans to redecorate the house to suit his own taste and needs. His vision was much more extensive than theirs, and as his second wife, Happy Rockefeller, notes, "He had a vision of the future, knowing that after he and his brothers were gone no one could afford to live in Kykuit. So from the moment he moved in he started to prepare it to become a public place." He also intended to make it his home, a place where he would feel comfortable and be able to lead a more informal lifestyle. Yet even when he removed wall sconces to make way for something more contemporary, he stored them carefully in the basement to be used again some day.

His first objective was to restore the furniture and fabrics as faithfully as possible to the styles and colors of his grandfather's day. At the same time he wanted to open up the interior of the house so that it felt more spacious and incorporate into its dignified, traditional setting some pieces from his own modern art collection. He had taken this eclectic approach in decorating his other houses, believing that truly beautiful things can live comfortably with any other beautiful things regardless of period or style. "I arrange the art of others in nice settings and beautiful places," he once said. "The enjoyment of a piece, whether it's painting or sculpture, whether it's in your home or in your garden, is a matter of putting it in the right setting or in the right combination."

Christmas 1955. Left to right: Mary Todhunter Clark Rockefeller, Ann Rockefeller Pierson, Sandra Ferry Rockefeller.

Nelson took great personal pleasure in all the details of this renovation; whether lining Sheraton cabinets with velvet or covering lamps with antique glass shades, his own strong creative instincts guided the process. He worked closely with Peter Ogden, a Connecticut architect, throughout the process. He often chose to use the back of an upholstery fabric because it was less shiny and the colors more subtle than the front. A sound system was installed throughout the house, with the controls housed in japanned cabinets in the front office, where the TV was also hidden behind faux bookshelves. He turned

a small pantry off the first-floor butler's pantry into a space to exhibit his collection of rare china, including Worcester, Spode, and Chinese export services, installing lighted cupboards and a round table on which to display the dishes. In the central hall he removed the old aeolian organ, which had fallen into disrepair, and used the wall space to hang a large, modern painting, Joan Miró's *Hirondelle Amour*. He removed the mirrored doors from between all the rooms on the first floor to let the light circulate through. Upstairs he chose to move into his grandparents' west-facing rooms, reclaiming the same primary relationship to the house that JDR had had. He installed a large plate-glass window in the sitting room overlooking the Hudson to maximize the breathtaking view of the river and valley. As his art collection grew and more space was needed, he came up with the idea of transforming the empty basement passages that lead to the grotto into an art gallery. Renowned architect Philip Johnson worked with Peter Ogden to redesign the space. So the spooky dark underground corridors we had dared each other to venture into as children became filled with light and a museum's worth of contemporary paintings, sculptures, and tapestries.

The exterior was as important to him as the interior; in fact he saw them as two parts of a whole. Knowing that the great old elms around the house were at risk of being stricken with Dutch elm disease and would one day be gone, his first act on moving into Kykuit was to plant four wisteria vines at the eastern corner of the house. Every spring he would check their progress and measure how far they had grown. His pleasure and pride were boundless when at last the vines began to cover one side of the great granite facade and turn the corner onto another. "One day it will really soften the house," he predicted. Today the elms are indeed gone and the vines are luxuriant all across the east and south facades of Kykuit, providing just the effect he had envisioned.

In 1963 Nelson's second wife, Margaretta Fitler Rockefeller, known as Happy, moved into Kykuit with him. As their two sons, Nelson Jr. and Mark, were born and grew, the changes and additions to the house and gardens continued. At Happy's suggestion a "flower porch" and snack kitchen were added to the north porch. She wanted a smaller, simpler, more intimate, and more accessible space than the big kitchen downstairs, a place where she and the boys could cook, arrange flowers, or get a midnight snack. The classical teahouse in the inner garden was turned into an ice cream parlor, the tennis court on the south lawn behind the stream was resurfaced, and two pools were installed in the sunken lawns of the inner garden. Nelson's great friend and the director of the Museum of Modern Art, René d'Harnoncourt, had suggested the pools to him, pointing out that they would reflect the sun, thereby increasing the sense of light in the garden and relieving its austerity. Thinking of his two sons and all his grandchildren, Nelson decided to double the benefit and make one a wading pool with a sand area and the other a swimming pool. In his art gallery he hung some of his sons' drawings and filled a display case with old bottles they had collected on the property.

To them Kykuit was home; their weekends there were a retreat from the relentless demands of the governorship and the eye of publicity. As Happy recalls, "We took the time for ourselves and tried not to let anything interfere with the weekend. It was a time to recharge, to fill up, and to rejuvenate.

Some fourth- and fifth-generation members at the children's table, Christmas 1955.

It's where we could all be together." They made use of every floor, room, terrace, and garden. The first floor became more and more an exhibition space, as Nelson's collections of both antique and modern art covered walls, tables, and cabinets, joining the art left by his parents and grandparents.

In spite of Kykuit's formality and the museum quality of much of the art, the family lived in a wonderfully informal way. They took meals in different places at different times. There were dinners with friends and Sunday-night family suppers in the dining room. Sometimes they had cocktails and dinner in the china room. "Nelson loved to show off his china," Happy remembers, "so Laurance said, 'Why don't we have cocktails here?' Nelson immediately arrived with a table and chairs." A tablecloth was added and drinks and hors d'oeuvres were served while family and guests admired the collections. Happy introduced the idea of buffet lunches on the porches because, as she says, "Nelson could barely sit at table throughout a meal without having to get up to do something or the phone would ring. And having two formal meals in that dining room was more than I could stand." In the winter Nelson enclosed and heated the west porch so they could continue to eat out there, retaining a sense of the out-of-doors and enjoying the splendid view. JDR's office became the family TV room, and Nelson often worked in his mother's drawing room across the hall or downstairs in the art gallery. The second floor was the family floor. "The two boys shared Abby's [former] bedroom," Happy recalls, "and her sitting room was turned into a playroom. Jr.'s study we made into a guest room for close members of the family." The third floor was for Happy's children by her first marriage and guests. The roof was where everyone congregated to watch fireworks on the Fourth of July or the stars at night. As Mark Rockefeller says, "From the very top of the house to the very bottom of the house it was all accessible. It was all used."

Nelson Jr. and Mark are the only two members of the family who actually grew up at Kykuit. They remember it as the place where they happily spent fall, winter, and spring weekends, many school vacations, and part of the summer. "It really was home," Mark says. "I think a lot of people would look at this house, at how big it is, and wonder, How can it really be home? But when I think back on it, it really was. It was a place where we felt incredibly comfortable." "The interior layout made it a very accessible, warm home," adds Nelson Jr., "with its modest entry, then two cozy rooms on either side, the spaces and rooms all linked together. We never felt lost."

The fact that there was so much art of great value in such an imposing setting did not impinge on the family's enjoyment of the place in the least. Nelson's firm view that art was important not because it brought large sums of money in the marketplace but because it was the expression of culture and the human spirit was passed down to his sons, who related to works of art as living objects rather than as investments to be protected from any interaction. "We really played among them," Mark recalls. When they were seven or eight they used to drive Big Wheels on the marble terraces, in and out of the fountains, and all around the front porch and the pools. "It was a terrific course," says Nelson Jr., "a continuous track, so you could go back and around and keep going. When you took certain turns at high speeds, the challenge was to keep from careening into the fountains. That was a lot of fun."

The circular lawn of the grand forecourt became their backyard, where as small boys they tossed footballs in the fall and baseballs in the spring. "We had home plate right at the north end, the pitcher's mound in the middle, and the outfield at the south end," Nelson Jr. recalls. "The whole goal was to hit the baseball over the stone wall into the garden. That was a home run. It is absolutely remarkable to me that we never broke the huge plate-glass window in the teahouse. We didn't hit the ball the other way because then it went way down the hill and we couldn't find it." Nelson would occasionally join the boys for a game. He also built a boccie court behind the shallow pool in the morning garden, and the three of them would often play the game together.

Nelson Jr. and Mark both tell tales of playing ball downstairs in the art gallery, with the large Picasso tapestries serving as backstops for the ball. "We used to go down to the galleries in the winter or at night and spend hours throwing baseballs back and forth. We played tackle football on the rugs," Mark recalls. "There were so many places to crawl behind and hide among and so many things to use in creative ways—it was almost like a gigantic jungle gym and we really enjoyed it." Miraculously, the art survived.

Like their father before them, Nelson Jr. and Mark had tasks to do around the house. "It was how we earned our allowance," says Nelson Jr. "Dad set up different chores that we would do both at Kykuit and in our New York City home. One was to rebuild the fires, another to shine his shoes, a third to vacuum our rooms and make our beds. I remember making the fires on the first floor of Kykuit. I also remember picking up Dad's shoes in his room and taking them down to the

Four generations on the porch at Kykuit, June 1957: Jr. and his second wife, Martha Baird Rockefeller; Nelson and Mary Rockefeller, Rodman and Barbara Rockefeller, and their two children, Meile and Peter Rockefeller.

men's hall in the basement. There was a big wooden chest with all the shoe-shine equipment. I have an old box with all these work sheets Dad made up. Each sheet would have Monday through Friday, and each task would be there. We would just check off which ones we had done on each of the days. On Sunday we would sit down with him and show him what we had done. Each task was assigned a certain amount of money. Then we had to keep our financial accounts, too. I still have all my old ledgers." In this way Nelson continued the long family tradition of teaching his children the value of work, money, and the relationship between the two. Many of the children of each generation have had variations of these tasks to do and ledgers to keep.

In addition to the art gallery, the basement housed the main kitchen, the staff dining and sitting facilities, and rooms set up for the Secret Service men assigned to Nelson and his family while he was vice president under Gerald Ford. Nelson Jr. and Mark were of course irresistibly drawn to them. "During the summer and on weekends during the rest of the year we'd have dinner in the main dining room with Mom and Dad,"

Four generations of Rockefeller men, June 1957: Jr., Nelson, Rodman, and the newest addition to that line, Peter.

Mark recalls, "and the first thing I'd do after dinner is shoot right down to the basement and just hang out with those guys. There was a Ping-Pong table set up, and I'd spend hours playing with them. Sometimes it got very competitive. We also used to bring our skateboards down to the kitchen and skateboard around the kitchen and down the hallways."

The lawn to the east of the morning garden became their vegetable garden. "We each had our own vegetable area to till," Nelson Jr. says. "Mom would work in her spot, Mark in his, and I in mine. Dad would be there with his. It was wonderful to be together but have your own area for self-

expression." Sometimes the boys sold the vegetables back to the house. This marriage of gardening and entrepreneurial skills was another family tradition. Nelson and his brothers and sister had cultivated small gardens on the hill just south of Abeyton Lodge, where they grew vegetables and flowers, some for the same purpose. David remembers feeling disappointed that because he was the youngest his garden was smaller than the others, and he could not grow as much. Undaunted, he decided to make his garden three-tiered so that it would triple in size. The problem was that the sun reached only the top tier, and the plants on the other tiers languished for want of light. Nelson and Laurance also raised rabbits, which they sold to the Rockefeller Institute. Nelson's children from his first marriage had gardens on the estate, too, near Hawes House, an early American farmhouse that Nelson had restored, furnished, and lived in from the 1930s to the 1950s, where they spent weekends and early summers. One daughter remembers gradually taking over her siblings' plots and growing a plethora of lettuces. When they were ripe, she piled them all into a wheelbarrow and trudged up the hill to her grandmother Abby's door, boldly asking if Abby would like to buy some for ten cents a head. In support of this young entrepreneurial spirit, Abby bought the whole lot.

Nelson and Happy continued the tradition of Kykuit as a laboratory for ideas and a refuge where work and play, business associates and friends, intermingled freely. They often invited close friends to visit for the weekend, and while he was governor, Nelson frequently held meetings with his closest staff at the house. As his parents and grandparents had done before him, he and his brothers used the original houses on the property to put up family members and staff who had become close personal friends and important advisers. Having family and other companions close by created a community of sorts, mitigating the isolation and loneliness of the estate.

When Nelson was governor, he would meet at Kykuit with his core staff in November and December to plan the next year's budget and legislative programs; he also met with his speech writers and other trusted advisers and staff. Sometimes he would have a whole team working on a single issue; he would assign each person a different aspect of the subject under discussion, and then place them in different rooms all over the house. On one occasion Oscar Ruebhausen (a lawyer, adviser, and trusted friend) was taken to Jr.'s former study and offered a wicker chair by a desk. As he sat down, the bottom of the chair gave out, to his great embarrassment. Totally unfazed, Nelson just proceeded to get another chair so the work could continue uninterrupted. "I'll see you in three-quarters of an hour," was all he said.

Very few large receptions were held at Kykuit because Nelson and Happy wanted to reserve the house for their private lives and cherished what family time they had there. The few exceptions included the annual Governor's Club reception to raise funds and an occasional Christmas reception for the staff of the family offices. They also gave several large parties outdoors under a tent set up on the tennis court: one for Nancy and Henry Kissinger, another for Nelson's seventieth birthday, and a third for another family birthday. For these parties little lights were strung along the stone walls and under the trees so the guests could wander through the gardens as Peter Duchin's music wafted through the air. It was like a fantasy come true.

Although Nelson and Happy kept large gatherings to a minimum, they took great pleasure in hosting intimate dinners at Kykuit for many of the business associates and personal friends they made over the years. These included world leaders such as President and Mrs. Lyndon B. Johnson, President and Mrs. Richard M. Nixon, and President and Mrs. Gerald Ford, and Ronald Reagan when he was governor of California. Mohammad Reza Pahlavi, the shah of Iran; King Hussein I of Jordan; President Anwar Sadat of Egypt; and Lord Mountbatten of England were also entertained. The artist Marc Chagall was invited to stay at the estate while he was designing the stained-glass windows for the small family church in Pocantico Hills, and both Andy Warhol and Spanish painter Joan Miró were visitors.

Nelson took great pleasure in selecting the dinner service for these events from the rare sets in the china room. His sons accompanied him, and they would discuss the relative merits of this or that set for the dinner at hand. Just before the guests arrived he would check the dining room, surveying everything with his exacting artist's eye, assessing the composition of the table arrangement, adjusting anything that did not please his view. He would sometimes get new ideas at the last minute and have the staff change the whole table setting in a great rush instants before the guests arrived.

Then there were the annual family Christmas parties, originally held by Jr. in his New York apartment and after his death by his daughter and each of his five sons in turn. When it was his turn, Nelson welcomed his entire extended family to Kykuit with great pleasure, his gregarious nature delighting in all the festivities. He had tables set up on the enclosed west porch and raised the large plate-glass window between the porch and the interior so that the family could move freely in and out before and after lunch. The old, formal Beaux Arts house became especially festive when it was filled with Christmas decorations, greens, flowers, and the sound of children's voices. The staff was dispatched to buy little presents for all the children, but one year, as Nelson was walking to his office in the city, he passed a shop filled with Polish crafts, dashed in, and bought every last present himself.

Nelson's greatest recreation and source of renewal was in acquiring and tending to his art collection, arranging and rearranging the works in their settings, whether inside or outside his houses. He had chosen early on not to follow his leanings toward architecture as a profession, so his art collection gave his artistic gifts a means of expression. As he often said, "Art has been an integral part of my life . . . because the enrichment and the spiritual as well as the aesthetic values that derive from it are incomparable." It was as though he was creating pictures or architectural compositions with the works in his collection rather than with paints or building materials.

Whenever he arrived at Kykuit he would go from room to room, readjusting the objects or creating whole new compositions. The staff was responsible for maintaining his arrangements, whether it was the furniture in a room, small objects on a side table, or the contents of the china cupboards. They would take Polaroids so that after dusting or cleaning everything could be put back just as it had been. In order to acquire new works, he amassed art gallery catalogs, auction catalogs, and art journals and magazines published in the United States and Europe, as he rarely had time to visit galleries in person. He would send them to his staff with the corners turned down on the pages showing the pieces he was interested in. The staff would then go to see the pieces and ascertain their prices and availability. If the price was right and he was still interested, the piece was acquired for him. Once an artist became very popular in the market and the price of his or her work rose accordingly, he rarely bought any more pieces. His eye was impeccable, and his choices of china, oriental porcelain, paintings, and sculptures infused the house and gardens of Kykuit with the forms and colors of art from antiquity to the twentieth century.

He knew and loved every inch of Kykuit and its collections and successfully integrated his new collections into the original ones. His sense of color, texture, and composition allowed this marriage of the old and the new: a Miró painting over the sofa in the eighteenth-century-style music room, a modern sculptured wall hanging by Hungarian artist Zoltan Kemény over a Georgian bench with a richly embroidered tapestry seat. As Nelson Jr. says, "He integrated and included so many different expressions and traditions that it became natural for us to appreciate and be comfortable with such wonderful diversity as well."

His interest in the grounds of the estate was equally active. He had great respect and love for the property, just as his father and grandfather had before him, and he involved himself in every aspect of its care. On Saturday mornings he took a tour with Joe Canzeri, manager of the estate and Nelson's right-hand man at Pocantico, visiting work in progress as well as his favorite places, often with camera in hand to record the season, the view, or a newly placed sculpture.

There wasn't a thing that did not catch his eye; he knew the name and placement of every tree and every bush. To him, everything had an architectural basis, and he could see how the composition in any given location was off or could be improved, ordering a branch to be cut or a tree to be moved without hesitation. His memory was not only superb but photographic, so he knew exactly what he had requested and whether it had been executed according to his vision; if not, it had to be adjusted at once. Once he had a picture of what he wanted he pursued it until it was accomplished; for example, he decided that the pebbles on the paths should be the same soft color as the stone of the house, and he persevered until he found just the right ones.

Whenever a new sculpture arrived, there was great excitement as Nelson contemplated where to put it. "He seemed to have an eighth sense of where things should go," recalls Happy. "I don't remember him ever measuring—it just seemed to be in his mind's eye." "He had tremendous inner self-confidence," says his brother Laurance. "He would just do them out of his intuition. There was great therapy, great solace, great joy to it." The new piece would be placed at the end of an alley, or among the branches of one of the great trees, or far across an expanse of lawn against evergreens, or perched on a wall with the Hudson as background. Each new piece would be moved until it found its ideal home. One day, as he was moving his sculptures, Laurance said to him, "Nelson, in a way you remind me of a shepherd with a flock of sheep. You gradually move them around." Nelson replied, "Nothing could be further from the truth. I am looking for the ultimate position for each one with the thought of never moving it again."

This search for the perfect site consumed him and often became rather complicated because many of the pieces were huge and challenged the capabilities of men, trucks, forklifts, and pulleys. If a stone or concrete base had been built for a piece, it had to be dismantled and reassembled every time the piece was moved, and the heavy machinery used to transport the sculptures tore up the lawns. All of this was enormously expensive. Not in the least daunted, Nelson kept looking for ways that would be both simpler and less expensive; he finally

Christmas 1963.
Top row, third from left: David Rockefeller; fourth from left: Laurance Rockefeller; ninth and
tenth from left: Nelson and Happy Rockefeller; sixth from right: John D. Rockefeller 3rd. Second row,
second from left: Ann Rockefeller Roberts; sixth from left: Abby (Babs) Rockefeller Mauzé;
seventh from left: Martha Baird Rockefeller. Bottom row, eighth from left: Mary Louise Pierson.

decided to do the moving by helicopter. A helicopter pilot and a rigger from New York who understood how to prepare and lift the sculptures were engaged. But well before a piece was moved, quite an elaborate process was undergone to select the desired location. First, Nelson and Joe Canzeri would go around together looking at different sites; Nelson would stand or sit in the places he wanted to be able to see the sculpture from, trying all angles until he was satisfied that he had the right location. Then Joe would mark the spot with little wooden stakes and approximate the height with bamboo poles. The next weekend Joe would arrive with a plywood mock-up of the piece itself. Again they would go out together, and Joe would turn the mock-up this way and that until Nelson was satisfied with its exact position on the site. Sometimes trees were removed or moved to accommodate the sculpture and frame it just as he wanted it. Only after all of this was done would the piece itself be moved. To spare Nelson the disruption on his weekends, the work was done during the week, overseen by his curator Carol Uht and Joe Canzeri. The piece would be carefully padded and tied, then attached to the helicopter with cables and moved slowly above and across the lawn. Finally it would be carefully lowered down onto its new resting place, positioned as closely as possible to the specifications Nelson had given.

One time his staff was in the midst of moving a very large Henry Moore piece called *Knife Edge—Two Piece* when they inadvertently ran into his brother David and a party of Chase Manhattan bankers on the golf course. Nelson described the confrontation at an awards presentation of the Council for the Arts in Westchester in 1977: "He [David] was having a party for friends of the Chase Manhattan Bank and I was moving this [Henry Moore piece] and you can't move these things except by helicopter because they are too heavy. So this [huge sculpture] came from one green where he was trying to putt over to the tee where he was then driving off, and this almost broke up our family's relationship because he thought it was planned. But it wasn't. The day before . . . it had rained and the helicopter couldn't come. And then somehow we didn't stop. But I am just trying to give you some insights into the joy of collecting or of having a collector in the family."

The fifth generation of Rockefellers was growing up at the same time as Nelson Jr. and Mark. Nelson welcomed his grandchildren at Kykuit just as expansively as his mother had welcomed hers. As babies they played in the same round pool in the morning garden; as they grew older they had the same freedom to roam about the gardens and fountains as he and his children had enjoyed, and of course there was now the added attraction of the ice cream parlor in the teahouse. "During the summer we used to sneak up to the gardens at night," my daughter Mary Louise remembers. "We would run barefoot through the cool, damp grass and then step onto the warm, dry stone in the inner garden. The only sounds were the gurgling and splashing of the water in the fountains. We made our way carefully through the garden to the ice cream parlor in the teahouse, opening the huge, heavy glass door slowly, so it would not make a noise. We searched in the dark for the freezer and then inside it for an ice cream sandwich. It seemed to us an amazingly dangerous and exciting adventure."

The fifth-generation members also came with their parents for the traditional Sunday lunch, except that the meal was now a buffet served on the terrace or by the pool, and everyone came informally dressed instead of polished up for a formal lunch at the great table in the dining room. There were Easter egg hunts in the morning garden and sometimes, as a great treat, the children spent the night.

Two of Nelson's older sons, Rodman (Rod) and Steven (Steve), lived on the estate with their young families for several years in the 1960s. Rod stayed in Hawes House, while Steve occupied a Victorian farmhouse, called Stevens House, next door. Both of these houses had been purchased by JDR when he acquired the land for the estate in the 1890s. Rod's and Steve's sons quickly joined the ranks of child-adventurers. "My brother, my cousin, and I would explore the gardens at Kykuit," recalls Peter, Rod's oldest son. "There was a sense that you shouldn't get too close to the house though. We would run through all the little paths in the Japanese garden, and we loved playing in the stream. There were two little piles of gravel near the teahouse, and we could not resist jumping on top of them and knocking them down. We had no idea that they were meant to symbolize sacred mountains in Japan."

Several members of the fifth generation remember spending the night in the Big House with Nelson, Happy, and the two boys. They could sink into the mystery and utter comfort of one of the canopy beds. My daughter Rachel remembers Nelson Jr. coming up to find her late one night when she was staying in a third-floor room. The two of them decided that, "because we were in this huge house we had to raid the fridge. We snuck down to the kitchen [the butler's pantry] in the dark and felt around until we found the fridge. When we opened it there was nothing there, nothing. It was empty. We didn't know that there was a huge refrigerator down in the basement with all the food. So we snuck quietly around the house instead, whispering and feeling as though we were making a huge racket. In the morning when we came down to breakfast, Grandaddy only smiled and said, 'Well, did you have fun last night?'"

Some of the grandchildren came on their own to explore, slip around sculptures, jump in and out of fountains, hide in the grottos, and play games of their own invention. To them Kykuit was "like a fairy-tale retreat," as Rachel says. They had the "freedom to play in so many places that were secret to all others," her cousin Sabrina Strawbridge recalls. "That was exciting." Rachel adds, "We looked at everything, we observed everything, and we knew each sculpture and the beauty of all the fountains. We would sneak around at night and just play in the shadows, we would sit on the sculptures when they were still warm from the sun. One time we went up and did a whole photography project, pretending we were the sculptures. We took pictures of ourselves standing next to these naked ladies and different sculptures, posing like them. Sometimes Grandaddy would

The Japanese garden, which dates to 1908, was part of William Welles Bosworth's overall garden design. This photograph was taken in the 1920s by Mattie Edwards Hewitt.

find us out there playing on the sculptures, and he would laugh and join in. I think he liked the fact that we were experiencing the art as well as enjoying it." Indeed, Nelson delighted in his grandchildren learning about art as they played around his sculptures, and he very much enjoyed having their laughing presence in his gardens and home. As Happy puts it, "Times change, and he in his own way did a little bit of rebelling against the rigidity of the period he grew up in. He was a free spirit and liked to be. He needed space and never objected to other people having space."

After he retired from politics in the mid-1970s, he had more time and energy to spend with his grandchildren. My son, Joseph A. Pierson, recalls a special encounter with him. "Some friends and I used to have camp-outs down in the woods behind the Coach Barn. At a Christmas lunch I told Grandaddy about them. He was very intrigued, so I invited him to come to the next one. To my great surprise, he actually took me up on the offer and showed up at the campsite on Saturday afternoon. He went through all the typical campsite rituals with us. We cooked him a hotdog on the grill. We served him iced tea, and we all had a wonderful chat around the campfire. As he was preparing to leave, he said, 'It was really nice of you boys to invite me down here. In return I'd like you all to be my guests at my ranch in Venezuela.' So that spring all five of my friends and I spent a whole week at his ranch, Monte Sacro. All this happened within a year of his death. It was during a time when he was finally stepping away from his career in politics and he seemed more open to his family. It was really very nice."

Nelson's vision of the future extended to the entire

Pocantico estate, and he was constantly coming up with ideas for projects or improvements. The Coach Barn, for example, was of great interest to him. Several years after Jr.'s death most of the horses were sold or given away, and the few that remained were moved to a smaller stable near the farm barns. So the stable side of the huge Coach Barn remained empty. Nelson was not particularly interested in riding or carriage driving himself, but he felt that the massive structure was part of the architectural history of Pocantico and that the carriages with all their accoutrements were evidence of his grandparents' and parents' time and way of life. So he decided to restore the building and turn it into a museum. He worked with Joe Canzeri and William Taggart, a former director of the nearby Lyndhurst estate and a great driving buff. They cleaned and renovated the stables, stalls, existing carriages, and tack. At the same time they began to acquire additional carriages, tack, and riding costumes to fill out the collection. They made replicas of the estate's original brass logos for the new tack, reproduced old estate

The Coach Barn, originally designed by York & Sawyer in 1902, was modified as seen here by Bosworth in 1913.

blankets and lap robes, and found an old fur driving coat. Glass-fronted cases were made to house some of the riding outfits and gear. When they were done the place was filled with all the paraphernalia of the coaching days, shined and polished and looking ready to be taken out at a moment's notice. There is even a model horse standing outside the stalls ready to be harnessed up for a drive.

With his eclectic love of all human-made objects, Nelson began to fill the car garage, on the other side of the Coach Barn's main floor, with cars both old and new. To him cars were another art form, and he collected them for style rather than mechanical interest or rarity. He also included cars that

had family history, restoring the early electric cars that JDR and Jr. had used, as well as the touring car that JDR took his daily drives in. The little two-seater Crosley Hotshot was there, as were several of the cars that Nelson had used as governor and a maroon Ford cabriolet that he used on summer vacations in Maine. The restored Coach Barn became a place of great fascination for Nelson's two sons and his grandchildren. Nelson Jr. remembers playing there for hours with his brother. They would go down to the basement to explore the big machinery and then up into the garage to play around all the cars. "We became big washers of cars," Nelson Jr. says. "We would wash the Datsun, the army jeep, and some of the other cars. I fell in love with Uncle Laurance's blue Corvette and remember saying to Dad, just on the side, how great I thought that car was. It worked out that if I took care of it, I could drive it around the estate."

Like their parents and grandparents before them, Nelson's boys and his grandchildren learned to drive on the estate. Several different small cars were used, but none outlasted the open two-seater Crosley Hotshot. There was a small Austin, a red Datsun, a small white jeep, and the famous retired army jeep, which Nelson bought right at the end of World War II. "We all learned how to drive," Mark recalls. "I remember Dad going out and getting me started. I remember going out to the middle of the golf course. It was very much the clutch and the first gear and slow with the gas and easy off the clutch and make sure you get this routine." Nelson was a good teacher, not easily flustered and very encouraging. True, one cousin remembers that he made her undergo a rigorous test of her abilities before she took her driver's test, but he was very easygoing about letting his grandchildren practice on the grounds of the estate. Inevitably there were some mishaps, but they were relatively mild, and the amazing thing was the equanimity with which Nelson responded to these accidents and the interest he had in teaching his children and grandchildren to drive.

The most famous driving incident involved four of Nelson's grandchildren and his son Mark. It has become somewhat legendary, and as with all legends there is some disagreement on the details. All agree, however, that the stalwart Crosley Hotshot was the injured car in question. The version here is based on Joseph's recollection, with help from Mary Louise and Rachel. Joseph was giving Rachel a driving lesson in the Crosley Hotshot. "The perfect car, I thought, and the perfect place because nothing could happen. The first mistake was that the lesson started on the hill leading from the Coach Barn to the Playhouse. She was going down an incline, which meant that she had to think about other things besides shifting, like braking and steering. But the lesson seemed to be going okay. Then cousin Peter arrived. He jumped in. The car is only a two-seater, so he sat on the back behind us. As we got farther and farther, the hill got steeper and steeper. It was clear that Rachel was losing control. She was having to brake and steer and clutch and shift all at the same time. She very quickly became incapable of doing any of it. The car was careening down the hill. The icing on the cake was that Mark, who was about twelve at the time and an accomplished driver, was coming up the hill. He and a friend were driving a little Mini-Moke, an Australian car, and coming around a blind corner pretty fast.

The Meiji-style teahouse was a central feature of the 1908 Japanese garden. It has been moved from this spot since Mattie Edwards Hewitt took this photograph in the 1920s.

A collision was unavoidable. Peter was thrown forward into the windshield, Rachel was in a panic and crying. Peter was bleeding, the Crosley was crushed in the front. Mark and his friend were both fine, the Mini-Moke suffered only minor fender damage. Peter was taken off to the hospital for stitches by my mother [Ann Roberts], who miraculously appeared. Rachel needed smelling salts. Someone helped pry the crumpled fender away from the wheel just enough [for the Crosley] to limp back up the hill to the Coach Barn. As Mary Louise and I drove the car in, who should be standing there in the middle of the Coach Barn but Grandaddy? He sees us and says, 'Hi, Joe and Mary Louise, how are you doing? It's great to see you guys.' Then he looks down and sees that his wonderful antique car is in a rather destroyed condition. Immediately his face changed to a dark look and he said, 'What the hell did you do to my car?' Mary Louise was thinking, 'Oh no, we're in big trouble now.' For a split second he was really angry, but as I told him the story his expression changed again, and he smiled and said, 'Well, as long as no one got hurt.' Now if you look at that little car, you would never in a million years guess what happened; they completely reconstructed it. It is really amazing, the whole car looks equally ancient."

Nelson loved the gardens as much as the art he adorned them with, and the Japanese garden was no exception. It had become quite overgrown since Jr. built it in 1908, and the Japanese character of the original design had disappeared. To redesign it Nelson hired David Harris Engel, an American landscape architect who had studied extensively in Japan and apprenticed with master Kyoto landscape architect Tansai Sano. Engel worked expertly with the original layout, following the path of the stream and the general contours of the hill. Within those parameters he created a beautiful stroll garden reminiscent of those in Kyoto.

The original mahogany teahouse, built in 1908 in the Meiji Temple style, was moved to a site below the garden within a grove of white pine near the lower part of the stream, where it resides to this day in harmony with its new surroundings. In 1961–62 Junzo Yoshimura, a respected Tokyo architect, was engaged to build a new Japanese teahouse. His traditional design was built in Japan, disassembled, and shipped to Pocantico. A crew of Japanese master craftsmen was brought over to reassemble the house on the site. They were quartered in rooms on the second floor of the Coach Barn and cared for by Helen Seo, a Japanese woman who had been in service to the governor for many years.

Engel extended the original path system and added new elements so that it was possible to make several circuits within the garden and never retrace one's steps or see the same things. One path leads to a waterfall and miniature gorge ingeniously constructed in the streambed, with the boughs of an ancient pine leaning over it. Stepping stones cross a small pool at the base of the waterfall, and the design is so arranged that the waterfall is completely hidden until the stroller is within the gorge itself. This path continues along above the stream, which widens into a pond. There the new teahouse nestles, its graceful lines reflected in the still waters. Another path leads through a dense grove of bamboo—where on summer nights moonlight shimmers through the rustling leaves—and on into a classic meditation garden, where the raked white sand and moss-edged rocks rest in silence. One of the original paths meanders both along and in the stream, allowing the option of watching the water burble along or of walking right above the water on the stepping stones. A low stucco wall topped with ceramic tiles runs along the western border of the garden, beautifully defining the edge while allowing views out over the surrounding lawn and westward toward the Hudson River valley. All these elements are laid out in such a way that they are concealed from one another by shrubs and trees and by

their placement within the contours of the hill. Full of surprise views and discoveries, it is an entrancing stroll garden that soothes and delights at every turn.

Nelson loved to walk in the Japanese garden with family and friends, but he also went there by himself to savor the peaceful atmosphere. Rachel remembers "skipping through the garden one day with Mary Louise and there was Grandaddy just perched on a rock by the waterfall, watching and smiling. It gave me such a feeling of warmth and pride in him and in his garden. I will always remember the expression on his face." He often used the teahouse for intimate entertaining. Dressed in her kimono and obi, Helen Seo would serve traditional tea or full Japanese dinners to Nelson, Happy, and their guests. Nelson and Happy often visited the teahouse by themselves, opening the sliding shoji screens on warm nights to the soft air and insect sounds. He allowed his grandchildren to use this calming, reflection-inducing house as well; they relished sleeping on the tatami mats and bathing in the deep Japanese tub.

The decor of the Playhouse came under Nelson's artistic scrutiny as well. He replaced the worn oriental carpets with new ones specially woven by craftsmen he had met while on a trip to Portugal. He placed pieces from his early collection of ethnic arts and crafts on tables in the living room, card room, and hallways. These areas served as exhibition spaces to him, allowing the retrieval from storage of some of the many objects he had accumulated over the years. He was an inveterate collector, and wherever he went objects of beauty came home with him. Happy felt that she was basically a powerless observer of this intense collecting activity, and she would watch in resignation as a steady stream of things came to the door. She remembers Nelson's first wife, Mary Clark Rockefeller, saying to her at a public gathering at the Metropolitan Museum of Art, "Oh Happy, these boxes kept coming in and I never knew what to do about them."

During the 1960s and 1970s the Playhouse was used extensively by the brothers, the cousins, and their children. As Happy noted, "All of the brothers were at their peak," and there were gatherings of all kinds every weekend and during the week as well. The events ranged from philanthropic and business meetings to family gatherings to personal events organized by individual family members. Business and philanthropic events covered the gamut of the family's interests, from environmental and conservation issues to education, the arts, health, foreign affairs, politics, and banking. Of the brothers, Nelson and David used the Playhouse far more than JDR 3rd, Laurance, or Winthrop. Both of them formed close friendships with many of their business and philanthropic associates. It gave them great pleasure to return the hospitality of their friends by entertaining them at Pocantico, making full use of all the delights the Playhouse had to offer.

Between them they entertained many dignitaries from all over the world. H. E. Felix Houphouet-Boigny, president of the Ivory Coast Republic; King Hassan II of Morocco; Ahmadou Babatoura Ahidjo, president of Cameroon; President and Mrs. Richard M. Nixon; British Prime Minister Margaret Thatcher; Prince and Princess Hitachi of Japan; King Bhumibol Adulayde and Queen Sirikit of Thailand; and King Hussein I of Jordan were among those who visited the Playhouse. Benny Goodman was asked to come and play the clarinet with the king of Thailand, who was very fond of jazz and played both the saxophone and the clarinet. The king of Morocco presented David with a set of colorful woven rugs, which are still in the Playhouse. David had large annual golf outings for officers of the Chase Manhattan Bank, including everyone from executives to assistant cashiers; Nelson entertained the state governors and covered the floor of the indoor tennis court to hold a huge reception for the Nixons. A large tent would often be put up over the croquet court right outside the living room for the bigger parties. Summer or Christmas outings were organized for the Rockefeller family office staff, complete with golf, picnics, and tours of Kykuit or the Rockefeller Archive Center, which is housed in the home built for Martha Baird Rockefeller after Jr.'s death. The number of weekend events ranged from twenty-five to almost fifty a year.

The family events held at the Playhouse included wedding receptions, birthday parties, graduation parties, coming-out parties, dinners with friends, and picnics around the outdoor pool. Meyer Davis and Lester Lanin, popular bands of the 1950s, played at several of the coming-out parties. Nelson, who loved jazz, brought Louis Armstrong to play at one of

his daughters' coming-out parties. Louis filled the tent with the sweet, intricate notes of his trumpet. And of course there were the annual family gatherings. Starting in the 1970s, the family Christmas dinners were held in the Playhouse living room, hosted by Babs and each of the brothers in turn, as we no longer fit into anyone's home. The Playhouse was also convenient for catering, and the Rockefeller family staff helped with the organizing. A festively decorated tree was put up in the living room, poinsettias and greens were everywhere, and there were always small presents on the tables for everyone. This tradition continues to the present day.

The fourth-generation cousins who used the Playhouse on a regular basis as children were the offspring of the brothers who lived close by or had houses right on the estate. Having no other neighbors, they were companions to one another, and they have fond memories of the Playhouse. "I remember swimming in winter," says Mitzi, "trying to make baskets in the gym, learning the billiard angles and sitting in those window seats looking out at the grass and trees between shots, bowling and playing croquet, watching my aunts and uncles and parents play round-robin tennis with their friends." The cousins spent hours in the gym, swinging on the rings, seeing who could shinny all the way up the ropes the fastest. They organized competitive bowling teams, getting better and better, and taking turns setting up the pins.

The outdoor pool, situated just south of the indoor tennis court, was built in 1955–56 and immediately became a summer favorite. Nelson commissioned his good friend architect Wallace Harrison to design it. They worked closely together, creating a design that was based on cubist forms rendered in three dimensions. One of Nelson's daughters remembers the saga of the pool well. It was intended to be an enormous sculpture, a swimming pool as art, a free-flowing form with several parts rising up out of the water, almost like icebergs emerging from the sea. These structures were designed to be used as slides, and Nelson's children and all their cousins were very excited at the prospect. The pool was also supposed to be painted several different colors. Cabanas were to be built along the south side, and a small kitchen and an ice cream parlor were to be installed on the decorative porches outside the indoor tennis court. When Nelson presented the design to his father for his approval, he found himself in the same position with Jr. as Jr. had been in with JDR so many years before. He had to persuade Jr. that a daring, modern design was just the right thing to complement the Tudor-style architecture of the indoor tennis court, and that cabanas and an ice cream parlor were not in the least too extravagant or indulgent. Even though Jr. himself had installed three beautiful swimming pools at Kykuit, again there was a clash between two generations with opposing tastes. Jr. had never been comfortable with modern art. Furthermore, the pool was partially visible from Kykuit, and he did not want to look at it because it was not in keeping with the more traditional designs of his generation. After much discussion, the pool and its amenities were built, but the two largest forms rising up from the water at either end were eliminated, and the pool was painted a single shade of blue. The resulting form is beautiful, however, and there is one remaining low slide that many children have delighted in using.

The Playhouse was very big, especially to small children, and the long, dark stairway leading from the gym to the indoor tennis court was particularly scary to many. Marion Weber, a cousin, remembers the feeling well: "The door [from the gym] leads to a dark hallway and at the end of the hallway are steps that go down. As you go down, the stairway turns. And you go down again and it gets darker and the stairway turns and you go down some more and then you can finally see a light at the end. But it's too scary and I think I remember turning back for years before finally going all the way to the end. And there at the end is this huge open space where the sound all of a sudden changes and it's light and there are echoes and it's spectacular."

The huge building had innumerable nooks and crannies, and as the cousins got older and went there by themselves, they devised many different games. Murder in the Dark and Sardines were two favorites. One cousin has memories of being packed into a small space with too many others at the end of a game of Sardines. Hot and squashed, she kept hoping to be found. Another was sure he knew all the possible hiding places for Sardines, but he did not see his friend hiding in the swimming pool under the diving board, even after all the others had gathered there. So he lost the game.

JDR's love of golf was not passed on to Jr., who is reputed to have said to his biographer, "I never finished a round." For all of his devotion to his father and attention to his wishes, this is one area in which he did not follow suit. It was his children, grandchildren, and great-grandchildren who inherited JDR's pleasure in the game. Steven Rockefeller Jr., one of Jr.'s great-grandsons, found and restored several fine clubs with his initials on them, and has them mounted in his home.

In the fall of 1934, as his daughter and sons were raising their own families, Jr. was persuaded by JDR 3rd and Nelson to completely redo the golf course. He engaged Toomey & Flynn, golf course designers from Cynwyd, Pennsylvania, to do a study and draw up plans and specifications. In June 1937 Jr. commissioned them to do the work, and the original twelve-hole course was expanded to eighteen holes over the summer and fall of that year. The work caused considerable disruption to the usually tranquil environment. As Abby commented to her sister Lucy, "The house in the country is perfectly lovely and I adore it, but John and the boys have turned the whole place into a golf course and while they were doing it, John thought he might as well have all the lawns around the house regraded, so . . . there we are surrounded by workmen and noise."

Nelson, Laurance, David, and their wives could often be found on the course on weekends. In early summer, golf outings with friends were often combined with lunch by the outdoor pool at the Playhouse. Nelson Jr. recalls his father's golf games with Laurance: "I remember Dad and Uncle Laurance playing golf; sometimes Aunt Mary and my mom would join in, but it was mostly just the two of them. It was one of their ways of visiting. They always played for silver dollars. Dad would have a stack of silver dollars that he kept in his bedroom. He'd take them with him and Uncle Laurance would grab his stack and they'd meet on the first hole. I think it was straight up—whoever won the hole got one dollar. Over the years things stayed pretty even, I don't recall either ever cleaning the other one out. I have saved Dad's portion of the silver dollars and the little silver-dollar holder."

Steve Jr. remembers watching his great-aunt Mary and

admiring her "as a very good golfer." He also appreciated "seeing Uncle Laurance and Aunt Mary playing golf together, well into their eighties," and loved "to see them hop off their golf cart onto the green."

In the early 1950s Nelson and Laurance brought in Archie Compston, a Scottish pro from Bermuda, to practice with them and to teach any of their children, nieces, and nephews who were interested. A tall, wiry, weathered man with a strong brogue, he believed in rigorous practice and in "sweeping the ball off the fairway." For all who chose to play, it was as much about experiencing how special the place was as about the game. "Playing golf was a wonderful way to get to know the trees," David Jr. remembers. "My balls went under them or at them a lot. It was a great part of my getting to know the property and the beauty of the place. The shrubbery, the textures of the grass, the contours of the land, and the views of it. I loved that."

In the late 1960s and early 1970s the fifth generation had its turn to discover the Pocantico fairway. "It is a magnificent design," remarks Steve Jr., yet "there is an informality about it. We often played without shoes or shirts. We even played with our dogs. It lends itself to beginners. You don't feel the pressure of having to hit shots in front of a huge membership." But more than the excellence and informality of the course, golf offered Steve Jr. a way to be with his grandfather in a very relaxed manner. When he was about thirteen, he "noticed that Grandaddy, Nelson Jr., and Mark were out there having the time of their lives. I felt that maybe if I played golf, I could make him proud and be with him. Riding with him on the golf cart was one of the great treats; you always got a series of terrific hugs and slaps on the back—it was very special. I can remember summer afternoons when it was really hot and we'd leave the pool up at Kykuit and head out onto the golf course. When he was vice president we'd come up over the rise and you'd see very quickly that we weren't alone, because the Secret Service people were always following in golf carts, watching at every turn and probably thinking they'd like to play with us."

Now members of the fifth generation take their own children out on the course on weekends or during the summer family gatherings. "Only last night we had a wonderful time," says Steve Jr. "We had three teenagers, we had my two sons, Stevie and Christian, and we had their cousin little Hunter, who is only six."

The golf carts used by the adults and their guests were kept in a garage near the Playhouse and were irresistible to the young as toys. Several cousins remember playing polo golf in them, riding them as if they were horses, taking them up the hill and then charging down to gather speed, while swinging the clubs to hit the ball, or driving the carts wildly over the golf course in hot pursuit of one another.

"It was great to have a vehicle at your command," says one fifth-generation member. "But you couldn't just take them out and bomb around. First we had to be chauffeurs for our parents and their friends. Then we had to pretend to be playing golf a little bit. Finally we'd all get in together, take the carts, and drive around the trails. They were all permanently dented from our escapades." Ingrid Rockefeller recalls "playing tag in the golf carts when we were kids. One day Wendy O'Neill and I were in one cart, Nelson and Mark chasing us in another. They hadn't found us, and we were flying around a corner to stay ahead of them. Just as we rounded the turn there were Henry and Nancy Kissinger out walking with their golden retriever right in front of the Stevens House. I slammed on the brakes, coming to a stop just about six inches from them. Henry looked at me and said, 'Whose are you?' I answered, 'Steven and Ann Marie's.' I was wild thinking about what was going to happen to us, but Dad never said a word."

Although the fifth generation of Rockefellers have had many of the same experiences at Pocantico as their parents, their relationship to it differs considerably. As children, most of them came to Pocantico for short periods of time, and to them it was primarily a place full of magic, adventure, and beauty. They felt very much at home there and did not doubt that they belonged. They had none of the confusion or discomfort about its riches and luxuries that their parents sometimes felt. "At the time I loved it. It was a wonderfully safe and comforting place to be," recalls a fifth-generation member. "From a child's perspective it was mine. It just was what it was." As they grew older their views matured and changed, and they began to see that Pocantico was different from their friends' homes. "I think I realized very early on that it was not an ordinary place," another fifth-generation member says. "No one else had a Playhouse or stables or things like that. It was an incredibly unique resource. We had access to just about anything by virtue of being members of this extraordinary family. Whenever I take people there, there is always an interesting mixture of pride and sharing in their wonderment."

Peter Rockefeller and his brothers and sister lived on the estate for ten years as children and adolescents. "Looking back," he says, "it was terribly isolated. People I know now grew up in much more social situations. It's not so much that you are locked in, but certainly the world is locked out. Also, it is so well taken care of that you feel that you are a guest here. There is never anything out of place, the grass is never too long. There is a level at which you cannot participate. You can visit, you can walk, you can do all the recreational things, but you cannot engage in the process of the life of that place at the level of fixing or changing. At the same time I do feel that it is a family home, and it is a wonderful, beautiful place rich with history."

The main caretaker of the Playhouse while the fifth generation was growing up was John Cinque—"Big John" to them. He loved children and took them all under his wing, admonishing them when they acted up and seeing to it that they did not go into the pool too soon after lunch. They spent hours in the pool playing Marco Polo while their parents held meetings around the edges. A trampoline was added to the gymnasium and used enthusiastically until too many children fell off and injured themselves, whereupon it was removed. Automated bowling alleys finally replaced the old hand-operated ones, and they bowled avidly. They brought their friends, cooked dinner in the small kitchen, played tennis, pool, and croquet, and went swimming. Ingrid remembers one special gathering: "It was a cousins'-weekend night—everybody was in town. I've never forgotten it. We sat in a circle and talked and played charades until four or five in the morning. The ages went from about thirteen all the way up to twenty-seven, and it was all family, all cousins."

Like their parents before them, they would sneak up in the dark to watch the fancy parties of their grandparents, lurking in the bushes lest they get caught by security guards. Rodman's son Michael remembers "sneaking through the bushes commando style while Nelson was giving a banquet for the president of Mexico." Another fifth-generation member adds, "We always thought we were being so clever because no one would ever see us. I'm sure they were perfectly aware of us racing around in the shadows. They just didn't mind." The fifth generation used and loved every part of the buildings and the grounds.

Suddenly, on January 26, 1979, the continuity of family life was broken. Nelson was gone, taken by a massive coronary in the night. Again Kykuit was to be empty, only this time there was no successor to move into the Big House. Nelson, Happy, and their two sons were to be the last members of the Rockefeller family to make Kykuit their home. Nelson's death marked another major transition in the life of Pocantico. By a provision in his will, Nelson gave his portion of Kykuit and the Pocantico Estate, including all the gardens and the Coach Barn, to the National Trust for Historic Preservation. The remarkable and extensive sculpture collection he had installed was included in the gift and was to remain part of the house and gardens. His express wish was that Kykuit be preserved and interpreted as a historic site "reflecting the lives of three generations of the Rockefeller family and their interests." Thus Kykuit entered the public domain; no longer did it belong to the family as a home. Soon after Nelson's death Happy, Nelson Jr., and Mark moved into a modern Japanese-style house he had built for them just southwest of Kykuit's gardens.

It was very hard for all of us to get our minds around such a radical change, even though it had been planned and talked about in different forms for many years; even though Nelson had held a formal dedication ceremony in 1976, with President and Mrs. Ford in attendance, at which Kykuit was designated a national historic landmark—the highest federal ranking; even though most of us were living elsewhere, raising our own families and living our own lives. It was still the family seat, the place of our roots, the home of our ancestors, and the thought of not being able to go there to wander about in the gardens or have lunch with our grandparents at the Big House seemed inconceivable. The thought of strangers taking tours through Kykuit was unbearable, too. One of Nelson's brothers even proposed tearing the house down rather than allowing it to become a public spectacle and a place where there was no longer family life. He felt that perhaps its time had passed and it should be let go, relinquished to history.

As it turned out, the act of giving Kykuit to the National Trust did represent a letting go, a relinquishing of the past; it was also the doorway to a new life for the dignified and historic place. The new life that has evolved has been deeply informed by the past, and everything that happens there now is in some form a continuation of the values that have been held and the events that have taken place since JDR's time.

The historic transition involved complex negotiations and arrangements among the surviving brothers as well as between the brothers and the National Trust. This process took nearly fourteen years and comprised several different stages. First, the property had to be divided. All the land and buildings were owned jointly by four of the brothers, Jr. having transferred ownership to them long before his death in the same manner that he received the estate from his father. By 1979 only David and Laurance remained, so it was left to them to decide which parts of it Happy and each of them would retain, and to define the parameters of Nelson's bequest to the National Trust. In 1983 they concluded an agreement with the National Trust that included the division of the land and buildings. The National Trust received more than eighty-six acres comprising Kykuit, its surrounding terraces and gardens, including the Japanese garden, the Coach Barn, and the Orangerie and greenhouses. This area was designated the Pocantico Historic Area to distinguish it from the parts of the estate that would remain in the family. This agreement also stipulated that David and Laurance would retain financial responsibility for the maintenance of the Historic Area, which would continue to be available to the family for philanthropic and personal use until such time as an agreement was reached

on the terms under which the National Trust would actually take over the Historic Area and open it to the public.

Arriving at what turned out to be a most complex agreement with the National Trust was the most challenging part of the transition. When a property is left to the National Trust the principals are often no longer living, and any remaining family members are seldom involved and certainly not living in the area or on the property. But in this case David and Laurance, the two living brothers, were very interested in the outcome of the arrangements with the National Trust, as were the fourth-generation cousins and the growing fifth generation. Their interest derived from a deep attachment to the place, as well as from a desire to see the family's values, as expressed through years of public service and philanthropic endeavors, carried on in the next phase of Kykuit's life.

The planning for this moment had actually been going on within the family since the 1970s and had its roots in JDR's conception of the estate. "JDR and Jr.'s concern was to form the estate, build it, and maintain it for their families as a family seat," David Jr. says. "That was really their gift. Jr. carried it out by building the Playhouse and the Coach Barn and allowing Nelson to build the modern pool. Then the uncles, under Nelson's leadership, began to realize that no one would be able to maintain the place after they were gone—it was beyond the capacity of the family to do. The message from the cousins was that then Kykuit could be and needed to be more than a family seat." As Steven Rockefeller puts it: "It became clear to most of us that these properties were unique, that their aesthetic, environmental, historical, recreational, and spiritual significance was priceless. Their location adjacent to an urban area with a population of over twenty-five million made them especially important. The family had both an opportunity and an obligation to find a way to protect and preserve this extraordinary heritage for the benefit of the community."

Conversations continued intermittently for nearly six years after Nelson's death; during that time at least seven different plans and proposals were brought forward for consideration by the different parties. Though it may appear to have been a very protracted process, in reality the extra time allowed for an important period of articulation and refinement. Eventually, the most essential principles became clear and were incorporated into the final arrangements, which reflected the visions and met the concerns of both the family and the National Trust. The family's desire was first to ensure the continued presence of the family's values through the establishment of a new philanthropic institution within the Historic Area; second, to ensure that the landscaped park surrounding Kykuit be preserved intact in perpetuity to the greatest extent possible; and third, to be sure that family participation and use were a part of any agreement. As the fourth-generation cousins put it, "We feel strongly that any effort merely to freeze the past would be a very inadequate reply, neither true to the family's record nor respectful of possibilities that address the future. . . . The right future for Pocantico will turn instead on what it might become in a vigorous new relationship to the family, one that is in keeping with the family's record of public service; and most important, one that will meet the needs and opportunities of America in a new century." This concern resulted in the development of new ways for the family's philanthropic interests to be realized in the Pocantico Historic Area.

The National Trust's primary concerns derived from its congressional mandate, which includes the obligation to ensure that any property it owns, such as the Pocantico Historic Area, is duly available for public visitation, that its defined standards of maintenance and historic conservation be adhered to in relation to the land, art, and furnishings, and that there be sufficient funds to ensure the implementation of this mandate.

Midway through the negotiation process the Rockefeller Brothers Fund (RBF) took on the task of facilitator between the family and the National Trust to work out the principles and details of an agreement that would incorporate both parties' concerns. Toward this end the board of trustees of the RBF, comprising three generations of family members as well as outside trustees, worked closely with the fund's president, Colin Campbell. Colin's now legendary ability to work through the challenges of coming to terms with the National Trust and craft an agreement that satisfied all concerned finally brought the negotiations to an end. The arrangements between the National Trust and the RBF were completed in

May 1991, and on September 30, 1991, the agreement was signed in the formal dining room at Kykuit. David Rockefeller Jr., chairman of the board, and Colin Campbell, president, signed for the RBF; Robert M. Bass, chairman of the board, and J. Jackson Walter, president, signed for the National Trust. David Rockefeller and Laurance Rockefeller signed over their share of the furnishings and art collections at Kykuit. Happy Rockefeller was present as a representative of the last family to live at Kykuit. As the press asked questions after the signing, David, Laurance, and Happy reminisced about their personal experiences in the old house, adding a human touch to the cool formality of the legalities. After the signing family members and RBF officers adjourned to the Playhouse and luncheon was served in the card room. In this way the legal transfer of ownership took place, and five generations of family occupancy came to an end.

Under the terms of the agreement the National Trust was granted ownership of the Pocantico Historic Area and its use for their own programs at their own expense. They then leased it back to the RBF, which assumed financial and managerial responsibility for the Historic Area, including the visitation programs and all maintenance, historic preservation, and conservation of the land, art, and furnishings. This arrangement was financially viable solely because of the farsightedness of several family members and the board and staff of the RBF. In 1976 the RBF received a very generous gift designated specifically for Pocantico from Babs's will. In the following years her gift was added to by the brothers and the RBF. From $15 million in the 1970s the Pocantico Fund grew to more than $43 million by 1994, and became the basis for the creation of the endowment for the Historic Area. The income from this fund allows the RBF to carry out its present role. David and Laurance then joined together and contributed nearly $8.5 million to construct a conference center on the lower level of the Coach Barn, to execute extensive restoration and renovation of the Coach Barn and the Big House, and to ready the property for public visitation.

As part of the agreement with the National Trust and in realization of the family's vision for a philanthropic institution at Pocantico, the Pocantico Conference Center of the RBF has been established, with offices on the lower floor of the Coach Barn. Its purpose is to further the programs and objectives of the RBF through conferences, seminars, workshops, retreats for the RBF staff, and meetings with other nonprofit groups. It is available to nonprofit organizations, both domestic and foreign, that wish to address critical issues in areas related to RBF programs. The upper floors of Kykuit and the Coach Barn have been altered to accommodate approximately thirty overnight guests. The Conference Center has been designed to hold some fifty gatherings a year of varying sizes, from small one-day meetings or retreats to full conferences of thirty people.

To carry out the visitation programs, the RBF contracted with Historic Hudson Valley (HHV), a local nonprofit organization. Founded in 1951 by Jr. and originally called Sleepy Hollow Restorations, this organization is well suited for the task. Its mission is to preserve the cultural landscape and history of the Hudson River valley and manage several local historic sites that Jr. was instrumental in preserving. The following guidelines for the Kykuit visitation program were established: tours were to run six days a week from early April until mid-November; a reasonable fee would be charged to allow the tours to be both self-supporting and widely accessible. The number of visitors was to be limited so that public usage would be manageable and consistent with the scale and delicacy of the rooms and gardens; the objective was to allow the highest-possible-quality maintenance of the Historic Area while ensuring minimal intrusion into the areas of Pocantico still belonging to the family. The plan was to start with 25,000 visitors the first year and gradually work up to a maximum of 70,000 visitors annually.

The period when all these negotiations and plans were in progress had an especially sweet quality to it for the family, becoming a kind of extended celebration, farewell, and leave-taking, although we did not realize it at the time. For the first time Kykuit was fully available to all generations. Previously there had always been a patriarch living there; he was the host and we were the guests. Now any of us could go there as we chose, whether for a meal, a celebration, a philanthropic endeavor, or simply a walk. So throughout the 1980s and until

the moment when Kykuit and the Historic Area were turned over to the National Trust, there was a great flurry of activity filling the staid, formal house. From January 1988 to December 1991, for instance, there was a total of fifty-one events at Kykuit and eighteen at the Coach Barn. David and Peggy particularly enjoyed using Kykuit and the Coach Barn for gatherings. Among many other events, Peggy, a dedicated cattle farmer, held a gathering of the Farmland Trust in the Coach Barn, David hosted a fund-raiser for the Museum of Modern Art, and Happy invited the Garden Club of America. To commemorate the 150th anniversary of JDR's birth in 1989, David and the staff of the RBF arranged a two-day seminar to bring together some of the organizations that had been funded early on by family philanthropy. All the facilities were used; meals were taken in the Playhouse gym, beneath a tent on the croquet court, and in the Coach Barn. Participants spent the night in the guest rooms on the upper level of the Coach Barn and at Kykuit. This forum provided a unique opportunity for the directors of these institutions and other participants to review their histories and discuss the trends and directions of philanthropy in the future.

The fourth-generation cousins and our spouses visited Kykuit often during this period, bringing our friends and associates. We felt a strong connection to our past as we sat once again in the main dining room, where we had shared so many Sunday dinners with Jr. and Abby, making use of all the beautiful china, glass, and cutlery they had lovingly collected and enjoyed. So we gave birthday parties and special luncheons at Kykuit, and we held our cousins' meetings in the living room, where we would sit on the same sofas and chairs, beneath the same pictures, as our parents, grandparents, and great-grandparents had before us. And like our ancestors, we organized events around issues and institutions that commanded our interests.

In 1983, for instance, David's daughter Eileen Rockefeller Growald held the founding dinner for the Institute for the Advancement of Health at Kykuit. "It had occurred to me," she recalls, "that Kykuit might be a really wonderful and intimate spot for bringing together scientists of very diverse perspectives in order to help them advance the field of mind/body health. On the first night, just as we were taking our seats for dinner, a streak of light came darting through the room from the setting sun and flooded a bodhisattva, the goddess of healing, set against the wall. Everyone saw it and felt it was a blessing of this moment and this effort. After dinner we went down through the art gallery to the grotto, and in an act of more playful intimacy one master epidemiologist undid the multiple locks on an old oriental safe only to find that there was nothing in the safe—it was completely empty. Everyone laughed and was disappointed at the same time. Later it became like a metaphor for what we were about to begin, reminding us that the treasure we were seeking was the connection between mind, body, and spirit and the power to heal through the integration of those three, and that we had to find that treasure ourselves."

On another occasion Paul Growald, Eileen's husband, took his parents up to Kykuit for a visit. As they stood on the roof looking over the great sweep of the Hudson, his mother mentioned that the Dutch word *kykuit* meant "lookout." "For me," Paul said, "that means not just looking out over the Hudson, but really being able to see the opportunities and possibilities that exist. My mother's father had the vision in 1934 to see the dangers of Hitler's regime and the strength to take action, to uproot his whole family, to leave his career behind, and move from Germany to Holland and later to this country. JDR and Jr. were both men of extraordinary clarity and vision. It is no accident that they chose the name Kykuit. They had the foresight to see problems, the vision to identify solutions, and the courage and dedication to take action and make a difference in the world. Kykuit was a perfect place to direct such transformative work."

The members of the fifth generation and their young families came to Kykuit knowing that time was short and that soon this part of their heritage would not be available to them. Like their parents, they organized birthday luncheons, surprise parties, and other special events that would leave lasting memories of the family estate. In the fall of 1982 my daughter Clare Buden arrived at Kykuit by horse and carriage to have all her wedding pictures taken in the south garden. In June 1989 her younger sister Rachel and Rachel's new husband, George Gumina, had their marriage blessed in Abby's rose garden. For the reception the guests wandered about by the fountains, enjoying the views and the sweet scent of the flowers. The christening of Abby O'Neill's newest namesake and a member of the sixth generation was held at Kykuit. Another baby was christened in the carriage wing of the Coach Barn amid the stalls, after which luncheon was served on round tables set up next to the carriages. Peter tells of falling in love with his future wife, Allison, on the west porch of the Big House as the sun sent its evening splendor their way. He proposed to her there in 1987. "We sat down in the living room on the couch and had a bottle of champagne. It was a historic moment in my life matched up with this special historic family place. It was a way of bringing Allison into the family history, of opening it to her."

Some fifth-generation members organized a series of seminars to learn more about their family history, the intricacies of investing, the mysteries of philanthropy, and business practices. One of the history seminars was held at Kykuit in June 1989; the topic was JDR himself. Several fifth-generation members researched his life, business, and philanthropic endeavors. They gave a talk and slide presentation for their peers; a large group of third- and fourth-generation members attended as well. This seminar was planned to complement the two-day 150th-anniversary commemoration organized by the RBF at the Playhouse the following October.

Often they came to Kykuit in small groups just to visit. "We saw many beautiful sunsets from the Kykuit porch," says one fifth-generation member, "while enjoying a pot-luck supper and the company of family and friends." "We used to go up there for the Fourth of July," recalls another. "We would walk through the art collection and really appreciate the house and then end up on the roof to see the fireworks." "We could see the display of lights from three or four towns at once," remembers yet another, "Tarrytown, Nyack, Pleasantville, and even White Plains." Sometimes they came just to walk around at dusk, drinking in the calm, ordered environment. "I loved just sitting up on the hill right by the putting green at sunset," says Ingrid Rockefeller. "It was one of my favorite things to do."

By this time the fifth generation had also begun to have their own meetings for business and philanthropy, following in the tradition of their parents, grandparents, and great-grandparents. During this period they held some of those meetings at Kykuit and took dinner in the formal dining room, savoring the magic of being in their ancestral house. As one of them, Jennifer Nolan, later said, "To me the beauty of the estate comes from a combination of its landscape and its history. It has served as a superbly beautiful meeting place for our family. It has encouraged and allowed our family to come together for five generations. The unique opportunity it offers to enjoy familiarity with one setting over several generations creates the sense of home we feel there."

The National Trust was to assume formal control of the property on January 1, 1992. A notice to that effect was sent out to all family members. On receiving the information, the fifth generation decided to have a final dinner in the Big House on December 14, 1991, the eve of the family Christmas lunch. It was the last family event to be held in the house. Following in the grand tradition of Jr. and Abby, the organizers sent out formal invitations to all fifth-generation members, and everyone came attired in black tie and evening gowns. Joseph Pierson described the evening's events: "We had it catered and ate a full four-course meal in the dining room. It was an extraordinary evening where everyone reminisced about their childhood experiences on the estate. I remember the catering staff standing around in awe. . . . At the evening's end, the last thing I did was to take a shower in JDR's bathroom. I had always marveled at that incredible shower with the millions of nickel-plated spigots, shower heads, and liver sprays. That night I took off all my clothes and marched in and took a shower." So they concluded their gathering with playfulness as well as formality, respect, and nostalgia. One of the fifth generation expressed his feelings later, "I walked through the art gallery and the gardens with the feeling that it was very much a living place, and just thinking how sad it was that it was changing. It was the end. It wasn't going to be a family house anymore. It was going to be a public place."

The next day the entire family converged in the Coach Barn for the annual Christmas dinner. All the carriages were removed for the occasion. Touched by the fifth generation's dinner the night before, we decided to go up to the Big House after lunch and hold a simple ceremony to say good-bye to the place we had known all our lives. All who felt called upon to do so gathered in the main hall, or music room. Standing in a circle of three generations, we voiced our memories and appreciation one at a time, lighting candles as we spoke, until there was a ring of light commemorating all that had been and was being let go. Then we left quietly, knowing that in a few weeks the house would be stripped of all its furnishings and a metamorphosis would begin that would bring forth another form of Kykuit, a Kykuit refitted and prepared for its new life in the public domain.

The preparations to outfit Kykuit and the Coach Barn with the equipment necessary for it to meet the standards for public access continued until the end of 1993. Smoke detectors and sprinkler systems were installed, security systems were laid out, all the artwork and furnishings were cataloged, and restoration work was begun. The third and fourth floors of the Big House were redecorated and refurbished as guest rooms. At the same time the large space under the Coach Barn stables was transformed into a handsome, state-of-the-art conference center for the RBF, designed by Herbert S. Newman & Partners, New Haven. The original staff rooms on the top floor of the Coach Barn were redesigned and redecorated as guest rooms for conferees.

Finally, on May 4, 1994, Kykuit, its gardens, and the Coach Barn reopened to receive their first public visitors. Eighteen people arrived in the first bus on that chilly spring morning after an orientation at nearby Philipsburg Manor. They were taken through the house, the gardens, and the Coach Barn by newly trained tour guides. The red velvet ropes and their stanchions were in place, symbolizing the final transformation from family occupancy to public visitation. Since that first day, the tours of Kykuit and the gardens have been sold out every year within a few weeks of their announcement. In 1995 50,000 visitors came. By the end of 1996 a total of more than 150,000 people had passed through.

The first conference of the Pocantico Conference Center took place in April 1994. By January 1996 more than fifty meetings had been held, and since that time the number of conferences and attendees has grown until there are now more applications than can be accommodated. The gatherings have included two United Nations working groups to address the challenges and problems facing the UN in the coming century, the first meeting of the Earth Charter Steering Committee to "prepare a document articulating a new global code based on the principles of sustainable development," and a two-day meeting on the contemplative mind in American society, hosted by Steven Rockefeller and his cousin Anne Bartley. The last day all the participants took a silent walk in the Japanese garden and then participated in a Japanese tea ceremony in the teahouse. "As we left the teahouse and came out of the garden," recounts Steven, "a helicopter came down and landed in the middle of the field between the first and second golf holes. As we watched in astonishment, the door opened and Nelson Mandela stepped out." Apparently David, his daughter Peggy Dulaney, and Colin Campbell had arranged for Nelson Mandela to have two days of rest and respite at Pocantico before his first American tour. "It was wonderful," continues Steven. "In terms of the transformation and new life of Pocantico, you had a meeting of the contemplative mind and the active life occurring right in the midst of this place."

In these ways the vitality that the family desired is being maintained; it is not a static or lifeless monument but an ongoing work in progress. The gathering of men and women to address major issues of our time, to explore ways of renewing and protecting our society and the earth we live on, continues the traditions and values set forth by JDR and Jr.

David Rockefeller Jr. described some of these values with precision and feeling in 1993: "The land, the buildings, the activities that take place there speak clearly of the values which have guided the family for a hundred years: respect for Nature as the incubator of life, as an emblem of physical beauty, and as a place for reflection, restoration, and recreation; respect for the built environment, including architecture, interior design and landscape design; respect for the diversity of humankind and human opinion; respect for the role of philanthropy and the non-profit sector in American life; respect for the power of 'Family' as expressed by a tradition of large and small family gatherings throughout the year."

On the remaining privately held acres of the Pocantico estate, the family continues to gather at Christmastime and in the summer. The Playhouse has replaced Kykuit as the symbolic center and gathering place, and the schedule is as busy as ever. From the first moment they saw it nearly a century ago, JDR and Jr. were drawn to this beautiful place, and as they built their homes and designed the landscape they became attached to the land. That attachment has continued through the generations. A cousin perhaps expressed it best: "I always feel I am coming home as I go through the great iron gates. The beauty of the tall trees, the stretches of lawn, and the serene view of the river engulf me with a sense of peace. My roots are there."

THE
BIG HOUSE

KYKUIT WAS BUILT in the early decades of the twentieth century as a refuge from the rigors of city life. A four-story structure in the Beaux Arts style, it is constructed of locally quarried rough-cut fieldstone and Indiana limestone. The first version of the house, completed in 1909, had steep gabled roofs, and the first floor was encircled by an open Colonial Revival porch. The architects were William A. Delano (1874–1960) and Chester H. Aldrich (1871–1940). The interiors were designed by Ogden Codman (1863–1951), and the gardens by William Welles Bosworth (1869–1966).

Dissatisfaction with technical elements of the first design—flues that did not draw, cramped third-floor quarters, and noise from the elevator and the service entrance, which had unwisely been placed below the dining room and master suite—led to the redesign of the house between 1911 and 1913. While the first floor remained largely

An early view, c. 1909, of the tearoom, or alcove, which opens onto the west porch and overlooks the Hudson and the Palisades beyond.

unchanged, the eastern facade of the upper floors was extended over the porch and a sitting room was added to the front of the house on the second floor. The third floor lost its gables and thus became more spacious, and a new fourth floor provided three rooms for children, a sitting room, and staff quarters; a tunnel leading to the basement level accommodated deliveries.

This second version was designed by committee. In March 1911 John D. Rockefeller Jr. wrote his father that the new layout derived from a conference and drawings by Aldrich, Bosworth, and Codman: "All agree that these changes are very desirable and will result in a house far more dignified and in much better proportion than the present house." This collaboration produced a Beaux Arts structure—an eclectic architectural interpretation of the classicism of Greece and Rome. Bosworth designed the new facade and recommended the extension of the forecourt to balance the new, more imposing scheme. A true classicist, he borrowed from many antique sources in both his garden and architectural plans. The facade, carved by the sculptor François-Michel-Louis Tonetti (1863–1920), is replete with allegorical figures from classical mythology. Reclining in the Palladian pediment are Apollo, symbolizing the arts, and Demeter, representing agriculture. Within vertical panels between the windows are symbols for the arts (a Doric capital and column with compass and rule, an artist's palette, a lyre, and pipes), and the implements of agriculture (a basket overflowing with fruit, a beehive, a sheaf of wheat with a scythe). In front of the porte-cochere, with its elaborate scrolling bronze supports by Tiffany, a grouping of five vases flanked by torchères with favrile glass flames is modeled on one from Hadrian's villa. Classical ornamentation, including acanthus leaves, roses, laurel, shells, and swags, adorns all of the bronze work—the grillwork openings on the porch, the balconies at the windows, and the railing around the roof—much of it made by Tiffany.

French doors open to the porch on all sides, allowing the gardens and landscape to become extensions of the interior spaces. Sunlight streams in throughout the day; the full vista of the Hudson and the Palisades to the west can be viewed from the library, alcove, and dining room, which form the widest part of the T-shaped floor plan. To the south of the library an allée of lindens lines the marble path leading to a classical temple that encloses a marble Aphrodite. To the north of the dining room two rows of English hornbeam lead to the center of the rose garden and the Goose Boy Fountain, after Donatello's in the Pitti Palace in Florence.

At the time of Kykuit's construction, Ogden Codman was the leading exponent of the Classical Revival style in interior design. In 1897 he and Edith Wharton co-authored *The Decoration of Houses*. This publication called for a turning away from "aesthetic-style" interiors, which incorporated exotic motifs of Japanese and Moorish or Turkish design. Popularized by the designs of Louis Comfort Tiffany, Samuel Coleman, and the Herter Brothers, this style was epitomized by the New York residences of William Vanderbilt (built 1879–81) and Henry O. Havermeyer (built 1890), and indeed by the Moorish interiors that John D. Rockefeller had inherited when he purchased the 4 West Fifty-fourth Street home of Arabella Worsham Huntington (now preserved as period rooms in the Museum of the City of New York and the Brooklyn Museum). Jr. and Abby knew Codman

The music room in 1909, as designed by Ogden Codman. Although an interior room, light pours into it through French doors and is reflected in the many mirrors.

and were familiar with his work in New England; they brought him into the project. Codman's work was governed by the doctrine of stylistic purity and the classical system of symmetry and proportion; its ultimate intention was suitability. As he wrote in *The Decoration of Houses*, "Proportion is the good breeding of architecture. It is that something, indefinable to the unprofessional eye, which gives repose and distinction to a room . . . in its effects as intangible as that all-pervading essence which the ancients called the soul. . . . If proportion is the good breeding of architecture, symmetry, or the answering of one part to another, may be defined as the sanity of decoration. . . . The line, and not the substance, is what the eye demands. . . . The decorator is not a chemist or physiologist; it is part of his mission not to explain illusions, but to produce them."

Ogden Codman's rooms at Kykuit, comfortable in scale and harmonious in design, reflect the styles of several English architects. In the drawing room the fruitwood furniture with delicately painted designs is reminiscent of the style of Thomas Sheraton, and the pale cream walls, robin's-egg blue ceiling, and classical moldings recall the work of Robert Adam. In the music room the proportions of the oculus, balustrade, and central chandelier parallel those in the central hall of Ashburnham House (c. 1662) outside London, which is attributed to John Webb, a student of Inigo Jones. The dome above the oculus was designed to carry the music of the aeolian organ throughout the interiors. The library, alcove, and dining room echo elements of the eighteenth-century English classicism of William Kent, and the furnishings, although primarily made for the house, are also in the eighteenth-century English style. Some pieces are truly antique, from leading dealers in New York and Boston, such as Frank Partridge, Joseph Duveen, Charles & Company, Stair & Andrew, Inc., and Koopman & Co.; and some were made in the early twentieth century by such firms as Tiffany Studios and William Baumgarten. The Chippendale-style dining room table, for example, was commissioned for the room from William Baumgarten, as were the dining chairs. In addition to providing many of the furnishings, Baumgarten was responsible for executing the elaborate plaster work of the interiors.

Jr. was closely involved in the details of the design, as one can deduce from William Baumgarten's letter of July 1, 1909, to the Monsieurs Hamot in Paris about the suite of Savonnerie carpets for the library, dining room, and alcove:

[I] have only just been able to see our client in reference. . . . He finds very decided objection to the light rose ground, and has decided that the plain center should be of the same tone as the shade of the deep rose ground marked "A" in the border . . . the outside border "B" should be of the same general tone of rose as "A" only darker and we leave it to your judgement to get the right effect. . . . The deep rose shade in the ornament of the border should not be as startling as the sample you sent over, but should be of the same tone as the outside border "B." (Codman Papers, Department of Prints and Photographs, Metropolitan Museum of Art)

Jr.'s attention to detail extended to choosing the cords for the blinds and the tint of pink for the color of the telephone message slips.

The Rockefellers relied on Codman's scouting in France for accoutrements to complement the interiors, and their correspondence provides a window into the process of finishing the house. For example, on September 14, 1908, Jr. wrote to Codman:

Father's new house is practically finished, in so far as is possible until your return. Almost all of the furniture thus far purchased is in place and the greater number of curtains will be hung this week. We find the house most satisfactory in every way. Those friends who have seen it thus far are enthusiastic regarding it. . . . We want to have these things in the house on the first of October, which I now hope will be possible in view of your cable stating that they will be shipped this week. Of course there are many things which still require to be bought for the house.

Mrs. Rockefeller and I feel your absence most seriously. Mr. Baumgarten is also abroad, as you perhaps know, so that we are quite helpless. We are hoping that it is your plan to return to New York in the very near future so that we can proceed as rapidly as possible to secure the furnishings and ornaments so necessary to give the house the homelike touch which you and we are desirous that it shall have. (Codman Papers, Department of Prints and Photographs, Metropolitan Museum of Art)

On September 26 Codman replied,

Dear Mr. Rockefeller,

Yours of the 14th reached me yesterday, and I am delighted that you find the house so satisfactory. I wish I were there to help you arrange the furniture, pictures, etc. I should enjoy doing so very much, as in that way I am often able to give the rooms I decorate the air of livableness I like my own rooms to have; but there will be plenty of time for that on my return; and by then you will have had time to see just what the rooms lack, and I shall have many suggestions to make.

Mrs. Codman and I have been very busy hunting up things that different clients have asked me to get for them, and we have seen the greatest quantity of lovely things, both expensive and not expensive. She has been urging me to write to you to ask if you would not let us pick up for you a number of little odds and ends that the house will need badly and that you cannot possibly find in America, such as pretty clocks, mantel ornaments, ash trays, inkstands, cache-

pots and small ornaments to put about on little tables; vases for flowers, lace tidies, etc.

One of my clients took me to a shop here, where they have, at very moderate prices, both in antique, and in reproductions, just this very sort of thing. (Rockefeller Archive Center)

And on October 20 Codman responded to Jr.'s letter of September 21:

Dear Mr. Rockefeller,

Yours of September 21st is at hand. . . . My experience has been that it takes a great deal of time and pains to get really good things, but that in the end it is well worth while. When one has completed a really beautiful and carefully thought out scheme of decoration for a room, in which all the furniture and objects harmonize, the pleasure that one obtains from the result is so great that one soon forgets all the petty annoyances. To obtain this harmonious result is what I have been struggling for ever since I started in my profession, but such have been the difficulties that I have had to overcome that I have very rarely succeeded in producing the effects I was striving for. . . . This result of harmony is what I have been striving to get in your father's house at Tarrytown, and you have been good enough not to hamper me in so doing. Perhaps you can realize how glad I am that so far you are pleased with what I have accomplished. (Rockefeller Archive Center)

Jr.'s aim at Kykuit seems to have been to attain the atmosphere of an English country house, with which he had become familiar and comfortable in his travels to England in his youth. In furnishing the house as a home rather than as a showplace of period spaces—a notion that would have been contrary to the sensibilities of both father and son—he demonstrated that he was as interested in function and form as in age or rarity. As Jr. himself remarked in January 1940,

I frequently said to the architects and decorator that my ideal for the house was to have it so apparently simple that

any friends visiting Father, coming from however humble homes, would be impressed with the homelikeness and simplicity of the house; while those who were familiar with beautiful things and appreciated fine design would say, "how exquisitely beautiful!" That was the result obtained. (Rockefeller Archive Center)

COLLECTIONS

While furnishing Kykuit, Jr. developed a keen and abiding interest in the art of the Far East, as evidenced in the splendid collection of Chinese ceramics. The first pieces of famille noire, or black hawthorn, ware were acquired as mantel ornaments, but Chinese porcelain soon became one of Jr.'s serious pursuits. In 1915, when the estate of J. P. Morgan was dispersed, Joseph Duveen offered parts of it to three collectors—Mr. Rockefeller, Henry Clay Frick, and Joseph Weidener—and Jr. approached his father for help in acquiring part of it:

I have never squandered money on horses, yachts, automobiles or other foolish extravagances. A fondness for these porcelains is my only hobby—the only thing on which I have cared to spend money. I have found their study a great recreation and diversion, and I have become very fond of them. This hobby, while a costly one, is quiet and unostentatious and not sensational. I am sure that if I had the actual cash on hand, you would encourage rather than discourage my development of so innocent and educative an interest. The money put into these porcelains is not lost or squandered. It is all there, and while not income-producing, I have every reason to believe that even at a forced sale I could get within ten percent of what these things would cost, while a sale under ordinary circumstances would certainly realize their full cost value, and, as the years go by, more. (Rockefeller Archive Center)

Ceramics in the music room and office were part of this early acquisition; Jr. continued to collect, and Kykuit is particularly rich in Ming dynasty (1368–1644) temple jars, garden seats, and figures glazed in deep hues of blue, aubergine, turquoise, and green, several in a technique known as *fa hua*. This term is often translated as "bound design," referring to the decorative technique in which a raised line of slip separates the colors of glaze—a method similar to that of cloisonné in metal. Equally well represented are the porcelains of the Qing (Ch'ing) dynasty (1644–1911), especially the richly detailed famille verte, famille jaune, and famille noire vases, many dated to the Kangxi (K'ang Hsi) period (1662–1722). Jr. was captivated by the exquisite craftsmanship and naturalistic depiction of myriad birds and flowers, and the beautifully detailed landscapes and figures. Rotating bases were designed for the larger vases so that the intricate compositions on all sides could be studied and enjoyed.

The earlier Chinese ceramics in the house, including the funerary wares from the Han (206 B.C. to A.D. 220) and Tang (618–906) periods, were added during Nelson Rockefeller's years at Kykuit. Han granaries, wellheads, and farm animals, Tang horses, camels, and guardian figures—all spirit objects to accompany the deceased in the afterworld—robust and powerful in their modeling, are displayed in the entrance halls, drawing room, and library.

The dining room is home to Nelson's collection of eighteenth-century Meissen birds. Massive white models of an eagle and a pair of vultures are attributed to Johann Gottlieb Kirchner and Johann Joachim Kaendler. Dated to the early 1730s, they were made for the Japanese Palace in Dresden of Augustus the Strong, elector of Saxony and king of Poland. The naturalistically painted polychrome models of kingfishers, parrots, African parakeets, and pigeons, which date to the 1740s, are also attributed to the prolific Kaendler, master modeler of the Meissen factory.

Nelson created the china room in the 1960s, combining three adjacent smaller spaces. In it are displayed and stored the dinner services of the house. English and Chinese export services from the late eighteenth and early nineteenth centuries are now in the collection. Worcester services include the colorful Kylin pattern of 1795 and the Stowe service made for the Duke of Buckingham for Stowe House in 1815. Spode

Newstone services include the King's pattern and the Ship's pattern, both decorated in the blues, orange, and gold of Japanese Imari. Four cases display Chinese export: armorials made for the European market; two services made for the American market about 1820—a delicately bordered Pink Scale and the orange and gold Sacred Bird, a dense pattern of birds, flowers, and insects; and two early services, an exceptional dairy service known as the Digby service, ordered in 1792, and a dessert service with the arms of Fane, the earls of Westmorland, from 1795.

The collection of paintings includes family portraits by John Singer Sargent, Adele Herter, Anders Zorn, and Frank O. Salisbury. In the library is an 1820 portrait of George Washington by Gilbert Stuart and an 1865 portrait of Abraham Lincoln by Joseph Alexander Ames; in the office is a late-eighteenth-century portrait of Benjamin Franklin by a student of David Martin. Two English portraits hang in the library: Sir Thomas Lawrence's painting of Mrs. John Gordon and John Hoppner's portrait of Miss Judith Beresford, which has hung over the fireplace since the early 1920s. An extensive collection of eighteenth-century mezzotints after portraits of the English nobility by Sir Joshua Reynolds, George Romney, and Thomas Gainsborough were acquired for the house by Ogden Codman, who fitted them with carved and gilded frames that he found in Paris.

Nelson Rockefeller enhanced Kykuit's formal spaces with works of modern art. There are sculptures by Auguste Rodin and Ibram Lassaw; a copy of *Hirondelle Amour* (1934), a lyrical surrealist composition by Joan Miró, now dominates the music room (Nelson gave the original to the Museum of Modern Art); Zoltan Kemény's abstract construction exquisitely reflects the dappled foliage of the tapestry seat of a Georgian bench; the luminous floating planes of Kenzo Okada's *Kozanji*, an abstract view from a mountain temple, elegantly mirror the distant cliffs of the Palisades across the Hudson. Glimpsed through the balustrade of the second-floor balcony are four paintings by American abstract expressionists and their European counterparts: Bradley Walker Tomlin, James Brooks, Pierre Soulages, and Karel Appel.

In the 1960s the organ pipe room and tunnels beneath

the terraces were transformed into galleries to display some of Nelson's collection of modern art. Strongly represented here are artists from Latin America, an area of continuing cultural, economic, and political interest to Nelson. There are works by Argentine Rogelio Polesello, Colombian Edgar Negret, Uruguayan Julio Alpuy, and Peruvian Jorge Eileson.

Several works came from the six "Americans" exhibitions at the Museum of Modern Art organized by Dorothy Miller between 1942 and 1963. These exhibitions focused on the state of visual art in this country and included the work of established painters and sculptors whom Miller felt deserved greater recognition as well as the work of artists then new to the scene who have since proved to have remarkable longevity. The art gallery at Kykuit contains works from those exhibitions by Robert Motherwell, Ibram Lassaw, Fritz Glarner, Grace Hartigan, Seymour Lipton, Richard Lytle, Robert Mallary, Lee Bontecou, Edward Higgins, Marisol, and Jason Seley.

A unique collection of tapestries after paintings by Picasso is displayed in the art gallery. Their creation was a project initiated by Nelson in 1955. He commissioned a total of eighteen tapestries—twelve are at Kykuit—to be woven after specific paintings. He obtained for each the approval of Picasso and the permission of the owners of the paintings, including the Musée d'Antibes, the Museum of Modern Art, the Tate Gallery, London, and the Peggy Guggenheim Foundation in Venice. (Nelson himself owned three of the paintings.) Skeins of yarn were matched to the colors in the paintings, where possible, and color transparencies of details facilitated the making of the cartoon, or pattern. The tapestries were woven by the Atelier J. de la Baume Dürrbach in Cavalaire in the south of France. All were woven of wool except the final tapestry of the series, after *Girl with Mandolin* (1910), completed in 1973; the delicate blues, grays, and browns of its cubist forms are enhanced by the shimmering quality of the silk used to render it.

Preserved as a period space of the 1960s and 1970s, the art gallery has been retained just as Nelson installed it. The arrangement of works of art was one of his great joys and talents; always in search of the perfect placement for each piece, he derived much pleasure from the hanging and rehanging of these spaces and from the installation of the outdoor sculpture.

Remnants of the past—the panels illustrating fables of Jean de La Fontaine that François-Michel-Louis Tonetti carved for an arbor disassembled long ago, the Mercer tiles left from the construction of the garden paths, planting plans for early gardens—continue to surface as reminders of the complexities of the original plan of the house and gardens and its evolution. Kykuit today reflects the tastes and collections of four generations of Rockefellers. Each brought favorite objects—whether Ming ceramics and medieval sculpture, twentieth-century painting and sculpture, or a collection of glass bottles unearthed in the nearby woods—to continue the legacy of Kykuit as a family home.

Kykuit sits high above the eastern bank of the Hudson River. Above: View from the south. Left: View from the east, with the Hudson and the Palisades in the distance. Right: View of the main facade and forecourt from the northeast; the inner garden is to the south (left) of the house, and the semicircular Rose Garden is to the north (right).

Elaborate wrought-iron gates and fieldstone gateposts flank the forecourt to the north and the south. Designed by William Welles Bosworth, they were modeled on those at Hampton Court. Each bears the monogram of JDR and a date; one has 1909, for the first version of the house, and the other 1913, for the second.

Right: The sun glances off the marble sphere atop the arc of scrolling wrought iron that crowns the gate between the linden allée and the classical temple. Below left: On a cold winter day the carved visage of Flora smiles from the keystone of the arched passage in the south wall of the forecourt. Below right: A wet spring snow clings to the branches of the cherry trees and the iron gates leading into the brook garden.

*View from the tennis lawn of the brook garden
and the south facade of Kykuit. A late snow
blankets the branches of the weeping cherries, the
rounded stones of the walls, and the raised arm
of Gerhard Marcks's bronze* Maja *(1942).*

In spring the weeping cherries burst into bloom behind the Japanese temple lanterns. In the foreground a carved head of Bacchus basks in the sun above a stone basin.

Opposite, top: Kykuit's east facade at the height of summer. Opposite, bottom: The west facade is reflected in the deep, still waters of the swimming pool. Clematis cascades from the stone bridge. Right: The west facade on a late winter afternoon; the sculpture on the middle terrace is sheathed in its winter cover. In the foreground a sixteenth-century stone triton holds a pipe to its mouth.

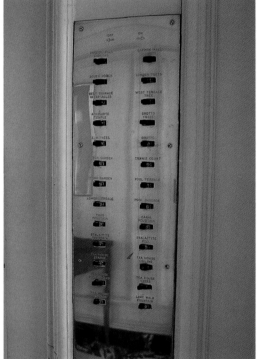

Left: View from the front porch of the illuminated Oceanus Fountain, flanked by the vibrant orange glow of the flame-form favrille-glass globes of the torcheres. Ming-style lions stand sentinel.

Above: One of the electric switch panels. "As to lighting—all of the fountains and water effects are equipped with electric lights, so that . . . the garden is as usable by night as in the daytime" (Bosworth).

Above: Glazed pottery figures from the Tang dynasty, including this guardian, were added during Nelson's time at Kykuit. Below: A collection of canes with handles of brass and horn, one carved in the shape of a panther head, with eyes of inlaid glass and teeth of ivory, stands near the front door. Right: Ogden Codman's restrained classical style is epitomized in the graceful proportions of the barrel-vaulted ceiling of the hall, the formal diaper-patterned marble floor, and the gilt-bronze lantern, similar to that in the stair hall of the Petit Trianon, Versailles.

With French doors opening to the south and east, the oak-paneled office was JDR's and Jr.'s favorite spot for their morning work. A painting of Benjamin Franklin (c. 1792), after David Martin's pensive portrait of Franklin in England, has been placed over the fireplace.

Favorite objects and family photographs remain as they were on the eighteenth-century burl walnut desk with corner chair. On the oak paneling above hang prints of two French financiers, J. B. Colbert and Nicholas Fouquet, engraved by Robert Nanteuil in the late seventeenth century.

K'ang hsi famille-verte porcelains from Jr.'s collection are arranged on a seventeenth-century French walnut trestle table. The mirror, with broken pediment in the eighteenth-century-English style, was made for the house in 1907. In a 1922 photograph, Abby is reading to her son Nelson, who sits with an injured leg.

THE BIG HOUSE ❧ 71

In the music room a copy of Joan Miró's painting
Hirondelle Amour *hangs on the wall where the aeolian
organ once stood. The eighteenth-century Chinese carpet
is ornamented with medallions, peonies, archaic dragon
scrolls, and auspicious symbols. The Ming dynasty*
fa hua *ceramics come from Jr.'s collection.*

The oculus and dome above the music room were designed to carry piano and organ music throughout the house. All the ornamental plaster-work in the house was designed by Codman and executed by Wm. Baumgarten & Co. The custom-designed gilt-bronze chandelier has five arms, each supporting five lights.

View of the music room from the second-floor balcony. Bradley Walker Tomlin's No. 5—1949 is one of four paintings installed by Nelson around this balcony. Glimpsed below it is a 1911 portrait of Abby's father, Senator Nelson W. Aldrich, by Anders Zorn.

The dining room overlooks the rose garden to the north and the Hudson to the west. The table extends to seat twenty-four. Frank Salisbury's portrait of Jr. (1947) hangs over the mantel.

John Singer Sargent painted this portrait of JDR in March 1917, in Ormond Beach, Florida. In June of that year Sargent came to Kykuit and painted a second portrait of JDR in more formal garb. On the table two pairs of eighteenth-century Meissen and Bow shepherds and shepherdesses surround a mid-eighteenth-century cut-glass epergne. On the sideboard are two massive white Meissen birds (c. 1734) made for the Japanese Palace of Augustus the Strong.

Detail of the eighteenth-century-style marble-topped side table. A lionesque mask holds floral and fruit swags in its mouth.

Left: Between the dining room and the library is the alcove. A Tang dynasty marble bodhisattva from a temple in the mountains near the city of Baoding, Hubei province, stands before the alcove window, which opens onto the west porch. Acquired in 1926 and displayed for many years in the Rockefellers' New York residences, it was brought to Kykuit in the early 1960s. After seeing the bodhisattva at the Royal Academy in London, where it was part of the International Exhibition of Chinese Art in 1935–36, Sir Percival David wrote, "This grand conception of the Chinese sculptor, full of grace and movement, owes much to the artistic heritage left by Greece and India to the Far East. It is from Greece that it derives the clinging folds of its drapery; it is India which has inspired the swaying poise of the body and its sensuous modeling. But it is the genius of China which has breathed into the figure its vitalizing spirit." The only other time the sculpture was publicly exhibited since its acquisition was in the early 1960s at the Metropolitan Museum of Art in New York.

Opposite: The library. The French doors behind the Tang Bactrian camel open onto the marble walk of the linden allée. On the south wall hangs a portrait of George Washington (c. 1820) by Gilbert Stuart. The Savonnerie carpet in shades of pink with ribboned border was one of a suite woven for the house by M. Hamot in Paris.

Opposite. Left: John Hoppner's Portrait of Miss Judith Beresford *(c. 1786) was acquired in 1924, and has hung in the library for many years. Top right: Joseph Alexander Ames's portrait of Abraham Lincoln (1865), one of the few done from life. Bottom right: A large Chippendale-style bookcase houses the library's collection.*

This page. Above: An enunciator panel in the pantry connects with rooms throughout the house, as well as with four locations in the gardens. Below: The china room, created in the 1960s by combining smaller rooms, displays and stores the Worcester, Spode, and Chinese export services. Right: The butler's pantry is just off the dining room. A dumbwaiter connects it with the main kitchen directly below; cupboards store oft-used china.

The master bedroom suite overlooks the rose garden to the north and the Hudson to the west. Today portraits of JDR's mother, Eliza Davison Rockefeller (over the fireplace), Laura Spelman Rockefeller (center), and Abby Aldrich Rockefeller (out of view) hang on the walls. JDR and Nelson used this suite as the master bedroom suite. Jr., however, chose the suite on the east side of the second floor.

Top right: During JDR's residence this portrait hung in the dining room. Bottom right: In the master bath hang prints by Cézanne, Bonnard, and Degas. The elaborate shower (Meyer-Sniffen Co., New York) has several shower heads and multiple faucets.

Above: On a side table are photographs of Abby and her three eldest children, left to right, JDR 3rd, Nelson, and Babs (1908), and of Abby's father, Senator Nelson W. Aldrich.

Above left: One of a pair of Bow candlesticks, each delicately modeled with a pair of yellow canaries, a nest, and fledglings among flowered branches and mounted on carved gilt-wood sconce shelves. Above right: The sitting room next to the master bedroom faces west, and the large central window overlooks the Hudson and the Palisades. Left: An engraving of Voltaire (c. 1778) hangs above a fall-front writing desk. Over the fireplace is an 1899 mezzotint by J. B. Pratt of the Hoppner Portrait of Miss Judith Beresford that hangs in the library. On the table to the left is a 1911 photograph of JDR.

Top right and below: Views of the northeast bedroom, once used by Abby. A dressing room lined with closets adjoins to the west. The suite of satinwood furniture is painted with neo-classical ornaments, strings of bellflowers, ribbons, classical figures, vases, acanthus scrollwork, and mythical beasts.

Above: The 1901 Davis and Sanford wedding photograph of Abby stands on a hall table. Bottom right: On the third floor are bedrooms that were for visiting family and guests. At the end of the center hall a graceful stair sweeps to the east end of the fourth floor, where there is a sitting room or library and three small bedrooms that were for grandchildren.

In the mid-1960s Nelson converted corridors below the house and terraces into galleries. *Above: Portraits of Nelson (1967) and Happy (1968) by Andy Warhol; in front is* Raumbug *by Spanish sculptor Amadeo Gabino. Opposite, top: In the foreground on*

the left are Louise Kruger's Bicycle Rider *(n.d.),* Fernand Léger's rug Blanc No. 8, *and above it,* Grace Hartigan's City Life *(1956). On the right is* Edward Higgins's Dinghy *(1960). Opposite, bottom: A transparent sculpture by Louise Nevelson sits*

above two casts from the Musée de Congo. Over the sofa is a work by Salvador Soria, and to the right a sculpture by Francesco Somaini, a print by Picasso, and a lithograph screen by Chagall. Nelson changed the gallery installations frequently.

The last of the galleries contain twelve of a series of eighteen tapestries after paintings by Picasso. This project was initiated by Nelson and undertaken with the approval of Picasso; the tapestries were woven between 1958 and 1975 by Mme. J. de la Baume Dürrbach in the south of France. They hung in Albany, Maine, and Pocantico. Left to right: Three Musicians (after the 1921 painting, woven 1966), Night Fishing at Antibes (after the 1939 painting, woven 1967), and Interior with Girl Drawing (after the 1935 painting, woven 1968–69). All three paintings are in the collection of the Museum of Modern Art.

Left to right: Night Fishing at Antibes, Girls with Toy Boat *(after the 1937 painting, now held by the Peggy Guggenheim Foundation, Venice, woven 1973),* Harlequin *(after the 1915 painting, woven 1968), and* Girl with Mandolin *(after the painting of 1910, woven 1974–75), the final tapestry of the series. All of the original paintings except* Girls with Toy Boat *are in the collection of the Museum of Modern Art.*

The grotto. Created when the gardens were built and located at the terminus of the gallery corridors beneath the classical temple, this is a fantastic and magical space, especially at night. Carved sandstone masks, antique forms recalling Roman theater design, top each of the eight sandstone columns. The arch system and ceiling tiles are Guastavino, the frosted green lights resembling clusters of icicles were supplied by Tiffany Furnaces, and the floors contain some of the earliest designs produced by Henry Mercer's Moravian tileworks in Doylestown, Pennsylvania. A Pan, one of three bronzes in this space by Emil Siebern, strides from a cave lined with coral and stalactite material imported from Genoa. The large wooden "Futuristic Flowers," added in the early 1970s, are based on designs created by Italian futurist Giacomo Balla in 1916.

Opposite and this page: The golf room, two floors below the dining room, is entered from the terraces above the putting green. This page, top left: The paneling conceals lockers for each member of the family. Top right: The sculpture (painted plaster) is by an unidentified artist. Bottom left: Glass negatives of JDR were set in the window panes. Bottom right: The shower, a less elaborate version of the one in the master suite, has needle sprays and multiple nozzles. JDR took up golf seriously in 1899 and had the course at Pocantico built in 1901 by Willie Dunn, an early golf-course architect in the United States. In 1937 the course was redesigned as a nine-hole reversible by Toomey and Flynn of Cynwyd, Pennsylvania.

THE
OUTBUILDINGS

The original stable building, or Coach Barn, as designed by York & Sawyer in 1902. Modified twice, once in 1907 by Delano & Aldrich and then in 1913 by Bosworth, when the steep, gabled roof was replaced by the flat one, echoing that of Kykuit.

THE COACH BARN

JDR and Jr. were accomplished horsemen, enjoying both riding and coaching, which were popular forms of recreation at the turn of the century. One of the notions of pleasure during the nineteenth and early twentieth centuries was rooted in the desire to return to the pastoral world, and driving excursions and country picnics were part of this quest for simpler times. Indeed, the network of roads in the urban parks of the last quarter of the nineteenth century, such as Manhattan's Central Park and Brooklyn's Prospect Park, was as much for carriages and coaches as for pedestrians. As a young man JDR became interested in driving and in racing light harness horses to show their speed and endurance. According to his son, "He was regarded as one of the best gentlemen drivers of trotting horses in New York" (Raymond B. Fosdick, *John D. Rockefeller, Jr.: A Portrait*, 1956, p. 10). The local press remarked on JDR's horses in 1891:

> *Flash and Midnight, owned by John D. Rockefeller . . . a perfectly matched pair of blacks, have been seen together for several years in this city. . . . Mr. Rockefeller is a consistent road rider, and except in the summer, when he goes to Cleveland, can be seen every day in Central Park and up the avenues, generally behind his favorite blacks.* (Harper's Weekly, *May 30, 1891*)

Jr. enjoyed coaching trips through England, New England, the Berkshires, and down the Hudson to New York City, and visited many resorts known for their miles of coaching roads.

uted by Detroit Electric Co.) was often used for short drives at Pocantico. Indeed, Abby's letters to her sons during World War II frequently refer to touring the estate in this car, a welcome alternative during the years of gas rationing. Four of the automobiles were made by Ford. The earliest, a 1907 Model S Roadster, belonged to Jr.'s sister Alta Rockefeller Prentice. Immortalized as the Tin Lizzie, the Model T was first produced in 1909, and a 1924 Model T was the first car owned by Nelson Rockefeller. In 1927 Ford replaced the Model T with the Model A; the 1931 Model A touring car in this collection is called the Rabbit because of the radiator cap, a gift from Abby. The 1936 Ford cabriolet has a custom body by the distinguished French coachmaker Alexis Kellner.

The 1939 Cadillac Model 75 four-door convertible, with windscreen for the rear seat, belonged to Jr. and was used in Williamsburg, Virginia. The 1956 Lincoln Continental, one of a limited number produced, belongs to David Rockefeller and was driven in Seal Harbor, Maine, for more than twenty years. Brought to Pocantico from Albany, the 1959 Chrysler Ghia was one of two acquired for use in conjunction with New York State activities when Nelson was governor.

Three small sporting vehicles are displayed: a 1924 Auto Red Bug buckboard (or Flyer), with a maximum speed of 25 miles per hour, is similar to the one used by Jr.'s children about the estate and village; later generations enjoyed the 1949 Crosley Hotshot, a doorless two-seater (one of several postwar sports models made by Crosley), and the 1966 Datsun 1600 red convertible, which was made by Nissan Motor Co., Yokohama, and is typical of the lightweight Japanese automobiles that would become staples of the American market.

THE ORANGERIE

Orange trees, originally from China, became popular in Europe in the eighteenth century:

In all the compass of gardening there is not a plant or tree that affords such extensive and lasting pleasure; for there is not a day in the year when orange-trees may not, and indeed

Jr. and Abby in the 1916 Detroit Electric on July 4, 1943. This automobile was used often during the gas rationing of the war years.

ought not, to afford matter of delight whether it be in the greenness of their leaves, or in the agreeableness of their form and figure, or in the pleasant scent of their flowers, or in the beauty and the duration of their fruit. (Van Ooster, The Dutch Gardener, *1711)*

Integral to the Mediterranean atmosphere of the Italianate gardens at Kykuit were tropical trees and shrubs—potted palms, oleanders, myrtles, bay trees, and several varieties of citrus. Early photographs and descriptions record four myrtles and six oleanders standing in pots by the teahouse and six bay trees in the greenhouse gardens; the pavilions near the swimming pools were, in William Welles Bosworth's own words, "flanked by sweet smelling old English jasmine trees in tubs, so large it takes twelve men to move them."

In 1906 an iron-and-glass-domed palm house and conservatory was built by Burnham, Hitchings, Pierson (predecessors to Lord & Burnham of Irvington, New York) to provide winter housing for the palms, bay trees, and oleanders. This structure was dismantled in the 1930s.

Bosworth designed the Orangerie in 1908 for winter protection of the collection of dwarf orange trees purchased in France for the gardens. Ten windows on the western side and six skylights above brought light to the trees within.

On February 17, 1908, Frederick Smythe of Wadley & Smythe purchased "an unrivaled collection of dwarf orange trees" purported to be at least two hundred years old from the collection of the marquis d'Aux at a château near Le Mans. Indeed, orange trees were among the most rewarding of plants, for they could bear flower, young fruit, and mature fruit all at the same time. In addition, as Jr. wrote to Frederick Smythe, "In those days the orange trees and bay trees added distinction and a sense of age" (Rockefeller Archive Center).

Three weeks later, on March 8, William Welles Bosworth was given the contract to design a "tree storage house at Pocantico" that was to be finished by September to protect this fine and ancient collection from the harsh winters. Thus the orangerie had to be built in haste. In design and proportion, if not in scale, Bosworth's inspiration was the orangerie at Versailles, with its tall, arched windows and plain stucco facade; even the boxes built to hold the trees, *caisses de Versailles,* were patterned on those used at the French royal palace.

Located parallel to the greenhouses and the former site of the palm house, the orangerie is a long, narrow building (interior dimensions 200 × 42 × 25 feet high; exterior dimensions 203 × 45 feet). It has a simulated stone facade of stucco with pebble-dash finish and a floor of "broken stone." Ten gracefully arched windows with terra-cotta keystones (15 × 8 feet) flank a central door of the same proportions. The windows swing open at the bottom from a horizontal hinge pivot, to provide air circulation. Wide, unglazed doors open at each end. The interior walls are white to reflect and thus increase the winter light from the ten windows and six skylights. Thick masonry walls absorb and hold the heat provided by the boilers, so that an interior temperature of just above freezing can be maintained. On January 18, 1909, when the outside temperature was a mere 2 degrees Fahrenheit, only one of the two boilers was required to maintain a temperature of 38 degrees Fahrenheit inside the orangerie, "all we cared to carry" (Rockefeller Archive Center).

In England and on the Continent, orangeries often served a dual function: in winter they housed tender plants and provided places to escape the cold weather and enjoy the fragrant beauty of the foliage; in summer, once emptied, they served as reception halls. Orangeries were first brought to this continent from England at the end of the eighteenth century, but surviving structures are rare. The earliest extant examples are in Maryland and Virginia, where the climate was close to that of England, and the plantations and architecture were often modeled on the English country estate. At Wye House in Talbot County, Maryland, the orangerie that survives was built between 1781 and 1784. In 1787 George Washington designed and built an orangerie at Mount Vernon, and correspondence reveals that it was based on the specifications of one on an estate near Baltimore. The structure at Mount Vernon today was rebuilt in 1952 from plans and archaeological information. An orangerie at Dumbarton Oaks, built between 1805 and 1812, is still in use as a conservatory.

THE PLAYHOUSE

The Playhouse was begun in 1925 and completed in 1927 by Duncan Candler (1874–1949), an architect who had designed the renovations and expansion of Abeyton Lodge, the Pocantico home of Jr. and Abby from 1901 to 1937, when they moved to Kykuit. He also worked with them in 1911 to expand the Eyrie, their home in Seal Harbor, Maine. The Playhouse was built just to the north of Abeyton Lodge as a place for the recreation of their six children, friends, and the many children of the generations to follow. The generously proportioned oak-paneled central living room has tall French doors that open onto a croquet lawn planted with floral borders, which change with the seasons. Eight family portraits completed between 1945 and 1947 hang on three of the living room walls: those of Abby, Jr., and their daughter were painted by Frank O. Salisbury; those of their five sons—all but Nelson in military uniform—by Edwin Dickinson.

The exterior design was inspired by the half-timbered buildings typical of Normandy, where Abby and Jr. loved to travel. Together with Duncan Candler the Rockefellers consulted the lavishly illustrated publications of the period, such as *French Provincial Architecture* by Henry Oothout Milliken and Philip Lippincott Goodwin. In fact, when Candler fell behind

in the schedule, Jr. wrote to him and urged him to take on additional help:

> *It is, of course, for you to select the man to work with you. In talking over the matter with Mrs. Rockefeller, she mentioned Mr. Milliken, who, with Mr. Goodwin, compiled the book on "Normandy Architecture" which you and we both have had and have studied. While I do not know Mr. Milliken, judging from that book, he must have a good knowledge of this type of architecture which would enable him to immediately enter into the spirit of our work and be of great assistance to you in promoting it. (Rockefeller Archive Center)*

For the half-timbered facade, oak was chosen over chestnut and cypress, which were also considered. Carvings of rams, wolves, and wildcats adorn some of the lintels and brackets. The exterior stucco, now ivory, was originally a pink tinged with yellow. Mrs. Rockefeller found rustic outdoor furniture in Cannes; ceramic farm animals—doves, hens and roosters, rabbits, and cats—in Bavent, Normandy; and pewter in Paris: "It will be a very nice occupation for you and me to polish it," Abby wrote to her son David on October 24, 1925.

Abby's lengthy letters to nurseries and landscape architects, including Wadley & Smythe, Frederick Law Olmsted, and later Arthur A. Shurcliff, attest to the care with which she planned the Playhouse gardens. The planting plan for the main court and front entrance included specimen English hybrid rhododendrons in various sizes, *Andromeda floribunda*, pachysandra, *Euonymus vegetus* for the walls, *Clematis paniculata* on the buildings, white wisteria for the entrances and pink on the buildings, and one large white-flowering hawthorn. In a letter of April 14, 1927, to Jr., Frederick Smythe detailed the planting plans for other areas:

> *[for the small gardens in front of the swimming pool:] 1,600 choice assorted perennials for the borders—These plants will include the choicest varieties of perennials and lists of same will be submitted to Mrs. Rockefeller. 20 Large Pink Ramblers, of the larger coarser flowering such as*

American Pillar; 20 Clematis Jackmani, for the front of the Swimming Pool Building.

Planting along the east side of the Tennis Fence: 6 Large Flowering Cherries, 4 Large Specimen Dogwoods . . . to be taken from the grounds, 240 Laurel, large symmetrical plants, 12 White Wistarias [sic] for pergola, 18 Large Blue Wistarias, on the building facing the tennis court.

For the Main Garden: 11 Large English Hawthornes (scarlet), 9 Large Standard Crabapples, 6 Standard Prunus Triloba, 18 Clematis . . . hardy English violets (280) in clumps and a variety of bulbs, such as Scillia, blue and white, and Lily bulbs of the finer Japanese varieties.

Along the building: large specimen Azalea Amoena and Mountain Laurel . . . Large Specimen Flowering Cherries . . . Large specimen Mugho Pines, dwarf, which will not obstruct the view of the garden and will also be effective from the lawn. (Rockefeller Archive Center)

To add something of her past to the Playhouse gardens, in 1929 Abby arranged with her brother Ned for cuttings to be taken from the lilacs of her childhood home in Warwick:

I appreciate very much you allowing us to do this, and perhaps some day, when these cuttings have grown up and you want to replenish some of your stock, we can return the compliment. I think I told you that I am starting a nursery of little seedlings and cuttings for the children, so that when they have places of their own, they will find waiting for them all sorts of young material. I am starting vines, shrubs and trees. (Rockefeller Archive Center)

Abby's involvement with the Playhouse plantings was but one of her many garden projects. In 1926 Beatrix Farrand was commissioned to plan the extensive oriental and English gardens in Seal Harbor, Maine, a project that was not considered complete until 1935; within a few years planning would begin with Shurcliff on the Colonial Revival gardens of Williamsburg.

Throughout the Playhouse garden there are medieval sculptures. A significant aspect of the interiors is the incorporation of medieval sculptural elements into the actual fabric of the building. The oak-paneled central living room, grand in its proportions, contains two massive fireplaces; above the mantel of each is an assemblage of fifteenth- and sixteenth-century French limestone figures of angels and saints, including Saint George slaying the dragon, Saint Margaret with a mythical creature, and a groom holding a steed with tasseled saddle.

In 1916 Jr. purchased a hundred pieces of medieval sculpture from the artist George Grey Barnard, whose *Hewer, Rising Woman,* and *Adam and Eve* grace the eastern grand stair of the Kykuit gardens. On extensive travels in Europe, Barnard gathered fragments of cloisters and churches that he had found scattered throughout villages in southern France—dispersed at the time of the French Revolution—and in northern Spain. He shipped these sculptures to New York with the intention of raising funds to support his own work. They were installed near his northern Manhattan studio in a structure that he called the Cloister; it opened in 1914 to great acclaim. Candlelit interiors, incense, medieval chants, and attendants dressed in monastic garb greeted visitors. Sculptures from this original group have been installed in the Playhouse and its gardens. In 1925 Jr. acquired a second collection from Barnard for the Metropolitan Museum of Art; these works are now housed in a branch of the museum—the Cloisters—that opened in 1938.

To provide a recreation center for their children, Jr. and Abby equipped the Playhouse with many facilities: a swimming pool, a gymnasium lined for basketball, a handball and squash court, a billiard room, and tennis courts. Toward the southern end of the building are the front hall and card room, which are hung with early-nineteenth-century English coaching prints acquired in 1925. Beyond the card room is the two-lane bowling alley—a long, low wing brightly lit by windows running its full length on both sides. Letters reveal much discussion about how to configure this wing to save the elm tree just beside it.

To the north, beyond the kitchen and the breakfast room, stairs descend to the indoor pool, an elegant, sun-filled room with French doors to the east and west. The blue-green tiled pool is bordered by a colonnade with Corinthian capitals surmounted by a frieze featuring eight roundels of fanciful sea creatures—sea horses, salamanders, lobsters, turtles, frogs, and octopi—and a barrel-vaulted ceiling. A small version of Barnard's marble sculpture *The Rising Woman* presides at the north end. Surrounding the pool are twelve palms in Mexican Talavera pottery urns on stands beautifully glazed in blues and greens. Indeed, all the ceramics, tin hanging lamps and chandeliers, and painted wooden chargers and boxes throughout the Playhouse were sent from Mexico by Frances Flynn Paine, the founder of the Mexican Arts Corporation. Created for the purpose of encouraging cultural relations between the people of the United States and Mexico through the exchange of handicrafts and fine arts, this organization was supported by Abby Rockefeller and by a grant from the Rockefeller Foundation. With Mrs. Paine's help, colonial furniture from Mexico was acquired for the restored houses of Williamsburg; Abby had written to her asking her to look for furniture brought to colonial Mexico that might be similar to that brought to the colonies on the East Coast.

On the second floor of the Playhouse is the billiard room with its great stone fireplace, Mexican tin hanging lamps, and wooden chargers. With characteristic attention to detail, Jr. wrote to Duncan Candler on March 19, 1927, about the choice of a billiard and pool table; not finding an appropriate one in the catalog Candler had provided, he came up with an alternative:

> . . . *whether this would be too elegant and rich for our billiard room you can judge. . . . These people indicate that they will make a table from special design. That might not cost much more and might be more appropriate. On the other hand, I am wondering how you would design a billiard table for a Normandy farmhouse. If you think you can improve on these designs submitted, why not try it?* (Rockefeller Archive Center)

There were two additions to the original Playhouse. In 1938 the indoor tennis courts were built. Incorporated into the large space were three large fireplaces and overmantel

surrounds from the Rockefeller home at 4 West Fifty-fourth Street, which was razed in the late 1930s; the land was given to the Museum of Modern Art for its sculpture garden. In 1955 Nelson worked with Wallace K. Harrison on the design of a modernist outdoor pool; it was installed that summer, with modifications of material and design suggested by Jr. in a letter to Nelson on July 5, 1955:

> *The Playhouse buildings are all of a very definite character and make a harmonious unit that blends into the surrounding landscape and is in every way pleasing. To undertake to combine with it what is proving to be so modern an installation and one that will be so conspicuous from the outlying areas, I must frankly confess gives me pause.*
>
> *To use materials that would be lighter in tone than say, bluestone, or some dull marble not more conspicuous in tone than the Boat Fountain at the kitchen entrance of our house here, would seem to me unwise. On the other hand, to use colors of that general type would, I feel quite sure, not be challenging in the landscape or in any way disturbing.* (Rockefeller Archive Center)

On July 11 Nelson responded,

> *It seems to me that your suggestion concerning the dark marble of the Boat Fountain is a brilliant one. I think it may add tremendously to the harmony of the whole setting as this color will blend harmoniously with all of the surroundings while at the same time it is rich in quality.* (Rockefeller Archive Center)

More than any of the other buildings at Pocantico, the Playhouse demonstrates the combined interests and collections of Jr. and Abby, from the medieval sculpture and French pottery and pewter to the coaching prints and Mexican handicrafts. Everything was acquired and incorporated with an eye toward creating a welcoming, harmonious environment for the extended family.

An aerial view of the Coach Barn from the northwest. The main floor is open to visitors and houses the collection of family carriages and automobiles. Visible from this vantage point is the new circular drive that leads to the main entrance of the Pocantico Conference Center of the Rockefeller Brothers Fund on the north end of the lower level.

Top: View of the east facade of the Coach Barn. The winter sun shines through the windows of the conference center on the lower floor and of the stalls and carriage room on the upper. Bottom: The south facade of the Coach Barn. The near wing now houses the carriage collection; the far wing, the automobile collection. Bosworth added the bell tower and the flattened "Italianate" roofs, as he termed them, in 1913–14.

Above: Gilt-bronze lanterns with panels of opalescent glass flank the massive doors of the automobile hall on the west side. Bosworth added the clock in his redesign of 1913–14.

Left: A massive stone wall forms a bridge to the carriage entrance on the south side of the Coach Barn. The stairs hugging the wall descend to a courtyard that was once for service and farm vehicles and is now part of the conference center.

The carriage hall. Left (from left to right): Road coach, A. T. Demarest, N.Y., 1892, patterned after an eighteenth-century vehicle; Roof Seat Break, Healey & Co., N.Y., driven four-in-hand by JDR and Jr.; wagonette, probably from the 1870s; six-passenger Glens Falls buckboard surrey, Joubert & White, Glens Falls, N.Y.; Gentleman's phaeton, Waterloo Wagon Co., Ltd.

Above: Gentleman's phaeton, Waterloo Wagon Co., Ltd., Waterloo, N.Y., of natural wood and complete with lamps, was driven with either a single horse or a pair. Left: Two parasol-topped park phaetons with wicker bodies, Van Tassell & Kearney, N.Y., 1902 (center and right); six-passenger Glens Falls buckboard surrey, natural wood with canopy, Joubert & White (left).

To the north of the carriage room are the box stalls and tie stalls of the former stable. Above: In the ceiling is the outline of the hand-operated platform elevator that once carried hay and carriages one flight up for repair or storage. Top right: Harnesses still hang ready for use. Bottom right: The spiral stair leads to the hayloft above.

Above and below: The door to the tack room is ornamented with a copper repoussé lion's head. Top right: Harnesses—double-set, single-set, and for four-in-hand—are kept in ready order. Bottom right: A corner of the workroom beyond the tack room. The case on the wall contains grooming equipment and veterinary implements; below it is a stool with a harness-stitching clamp.

The tack room stores English, Western, and ladies' side saddles. The display cases contain a variety of bits, including Ashleigh, Elbow, Liverpool, Buxton, and Pelham.

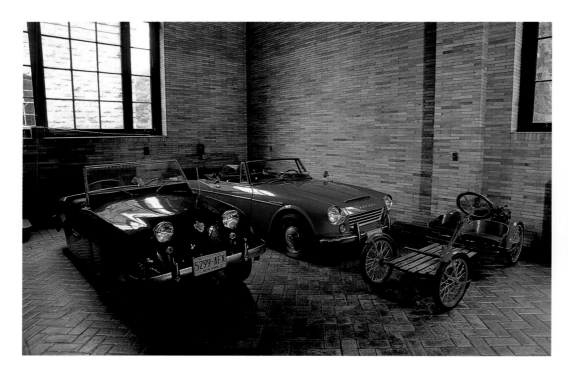

The automobile hall today houses a collection of twelve vehicles once owned and used by the family. Above left: Three sporting vehicles (left to right): 1949 Crosley Hotshot, 1966 Datsun convertible, and 1924 Auto Red Bug. Above right: The 1959 Chrysler Ghia, with license plate #1, used when Nelson was governor. Left: 1918 Crane Simplex Tourer (with phaeton body by J. B. Brewster & Co., New York).

An overview of the automobile hall (left to right):
1939 Cadillac Model 75 convertible, 1918
Crane Simplex, 1936 Ford Cabriolet, 1956
Lincoln Continental, 1959 Chrysler Ghia.

Above: To the west of the orangerie is a row of greenhouses. They have been used for propagation and for wintering annuals, some perennials, small citrus trees, and banana trees. Left: The interior of the orangerie, eerie today in its emptiness, once was the winter home of the tropical trees—oleanders, bay trees, palms, and several varieties of citrus, including, of course, orange trees—that graced the terraces and gardens. Right: The orangerie, designed in 1908 by Bosworth.

An aerial view of the Playhouse, designed by Duncan Candler and completed in 1927. Abeyton Lodge, the Pocantico residence of Jr. and Abby from 1901 until they moved into Kykuit in the late 1930s, once stood just to the west of the Playhouse.

Left: Designed in the style of the architecture of Normandy, the Playhouse has a stucco and oak half-timbered facade and a slate roof.

Opposite: The border plantings on the eastern lawns are changed seasonally.

Above: The lintel above the door to the living room. Left: The croquet court is located just outside the main living room. In the foreground a marble bowl rests on a column that rises up from the back of a lion, thirteenth- to fourteenth-century Italian, from George Grey Barnard's collection. Below: Wisteria graces the living room entrance.

Above and right: Glazed ceramic cats from a pottery in Bavent, Normandy, can be found scattered throughout the gardens. Ceramic rabbits, roosters, hens, and doves also appear in quiet corners, on walls, and amid patches of grass.

Christmas in the main living room. Eight family portraits hang on the paneled walls. Those of Abby, Jr., and Babs are by Frank Salisbury. Edwin Dickinson painted those of the five sons. Above the fireplaces at the north and south ends of the room are assemblages of French limestone sculptures, primarily of the fifteenth and sixteenth centuries.

The card room. The collection of early-nineteenth-century coaching prints here and in the halls reflects Jr.'s interest in carriage driving. The backs of the chairs were embroidered with floral patterns and initials by Abby. Hanging lights in the four corners are rimmed with a decorative band of spades, clubs, diamonds, and hearts.

The billiard room on the second floor has a high, timbered ceiling, a massive stone fireplace, and hanging tin lamps, some with painted glass panels. Lacquered wooden chargers from Mexico decorate the walls.

Bowling was introduced to the New World by Dutch settlers. Bowling alleys were not unusual features in the country houses of the early twentieth century. Delano and Aldrich's plan for the Big House included one (though it was not installed), as did Charles Platt's for Seven Springs, the Mt. Kisco home he designed for Agnes and Ernst Meyer in 1920. Here shoes in all sizes and Brunswick bowling balls are lined up ready for play. The two lanes are in a narrow wing at the south end of the Playhouse. Mexican painted tin and glass lamps light the lanes.

Left: At the south end of the pool, a tiled panel depicts a band of turbaned men presenting a fire-breathing dragon to a seated dignitary. Right: Four gilt-bronze crabs guard the corners of the pool. Below: The pool is bordered by a graceful colonnade and a series of areca palms in glazed Talavera pots from Mexico. The hanging lamps of brightly painted tin are also Mexican.

Sun streams through the French doors to the east and west of the pool. At the far (north) end, mounted on a pedestal, is a small version of George Grey Barnard's Rising Woman. *Two herms in satyr form stand sentinel to the east. In the frieze above the columns are rectangular panels with putti and roundels with sea creatures in relief.*

Above: The gymnasium is well equipped with exercise machines, ropes, rings, and a small trampoline. The floor is lined for basketball and handball. Right: The hall that leads from the gym to the tennis courts is lined with three late-nineteenth-century bronzes. At the end is a nineteenth-century academic painting of peacocks, geese, ducks, and other birds in a classical landscape.

Opposite: The indoor tennis court was added to the Playhouse in 1938. It incorporates lighting fixtures, three fireplaces, and overmantel surrounds from JDR's residence at 4 West Fifty-fourth Street, which was torn down to make way for the garden of the Museum of Modern Art.

Above: In the living room overlooking the indoor tennis court is a Tiffany gilt-bronze clock, also from the 4 West Fifty-fourth Street residence. Left: This fireplace and surround was originally in the front stair hall of the New York house. Above the mantel is a bronze relief of the goddess Diana in a woodland. Below: Detail of the mantel.

*Details of the elaborately carved fireplaces in
the indoor tennis court. Left: A winged hound,
seated, with a garland of pomegranates and
grapes in its mouth. Right: An ebonized female
figure among acanthus leaves and scrolls.*

In 1955 an outdoor swimming pool and cabanas
were added to the Playhouse grounds. Designed by
Wallace K. Harrison, the pool's modernist shape
recalls two submerged skiffs with bows rising
above the surface of the water. When originally
built, Jr. requested that it be of materials the
color of bluestone or some dull marble to blend
harmoniously with the landscape. The porch to
the left contains a soda fountain.

The tennis courts are located to the east of the Playhouse. Wisteria shades the viewing stand to the north.

THE GARDENS

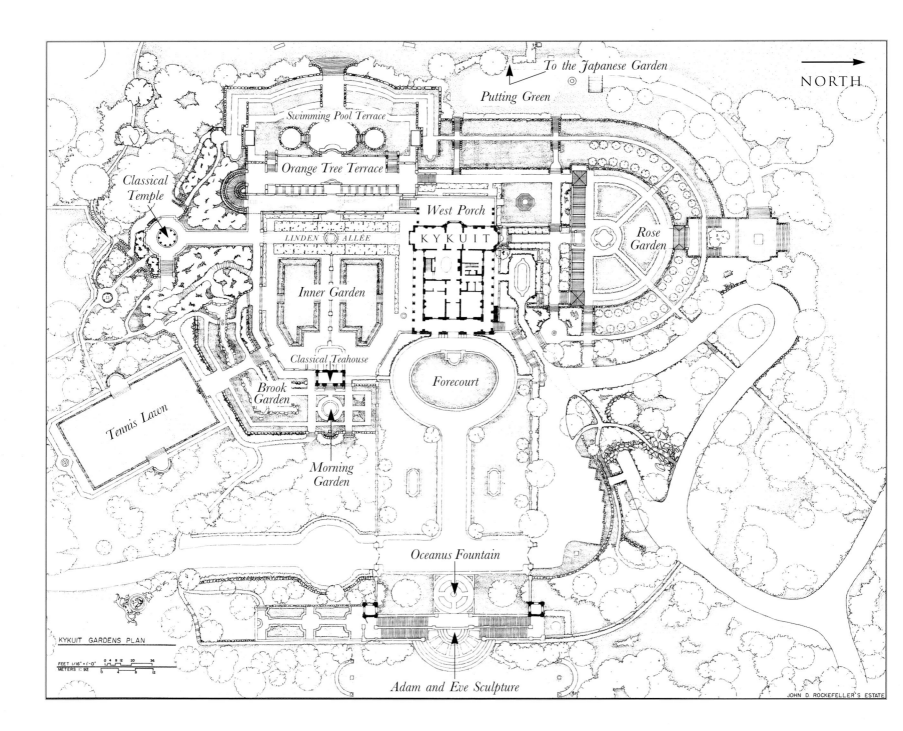

To the Japanese Garden

NORTH

Putting Green

Swimming Pool Terrace

Orange Tree Terrace

Classical Temple

West Porch

K Y K U I T

Rose Garden

LINDEN ALLÉE

Inner Garden

Classical Teahouse

Brook Garden

Forecourt

Tennis Lawn

Morning Garden

Oceanus Fountain

KYKUIT GARDENS PLAN

FEET 1/16" = 1'-0"   0 4 8 12   20   36
METERS 1:192   0   4   8   12

Adam and Eve Sculpture

JOHN D. ROCKEFELLER'S ESTATE

EACH GENERATION THAT had a hand in the design of Kykuit's gardens faced the task with its own vision. JDR was interested in creating wide vistas encompassing a bucolic landscape of rolling hills and gently sloping terrain—an approach steeped in the eighteenth-century English tradition, which emphasized the redemptive power of the landscape. Frederick Law Olmsted's natural landscapes in the late nineteenth and early twentieth centuries were grounded in this tradition. Warren Manning, a disciple of Olmsted, was brought to Cleveland in 1897 to work on JDR's residence at Forest Hill, and both Olmsted and Manning were called in at various times to consult on the plans for Kykuit's gardens. If JDR concentrated on the lawns, golf course, and trees—the groves of copper beeches, the transplanting of the full-grown elms and evergreens—Jr. focused on ordering the landscape in the more formal Beaux Arts gardens, reflecting the traditions of European garden design (especially Italian and French). Nelson extended that formality into a background for a collection of masterworks of twentieth-century sculpture.

The gardens at Kykuit were created in the early twentieth century, when Italian gardens were at the height of their popularity among American garden designers. William Welles Bos-

Designed by Bosworth, the south gateway to the forecourt was modeled after "the great gates at Hampton Court Palace."

worth, Kykuit's primary landscape architect, studied at MIT and the Ecole des Beaux Arts in Paris. He was steeped in the classical and Italian tradition; indeed, he spent some time in the London studio of Sir Lawrence Alma-Tadema, an artist renowned for his historical and allegorical paintings set in ancient times. In his work Bosworth quoted design forms—terraces, grand stairs, grottoes—and sculptural forms from such well-known Italian gardens as Boboli and those at Villa Lante, Villa Borghese, and Hadrian's villa. In an article about the

Kykuit gardens he describes the influence Italian garden design has had on gardens throughout history:

We have become familiar with the famous old gardens of Italy through drawings of Maxfield Parrish [in Edith Wharton's book Italian Villas and Their Gardens, *1903–4], as well as every sort of photographic reproduction. The Italian gardens being the origin of all subsequent garden tradition, and themselves a faint echo of the Roman Garden, the illustrated books and magazines have brought us down from them through the gardens of Spain and France to the nineteenth century English garden, so beautifully and profusely shown in the pages of the English magazines and to our own little efforts here in America. (William Welles Bosworth, "The Garden at Pocantico Hills, Estate of John D. Rockefeller, Esq.,"* American Architect, *January 4, 1911, p. 1)*

A long approach road from the village to the north encircles the house and winds gently up from the south. The forecourt is flanked by two sets of iron gates with fieldstone gateposts, which are crowned with carved stone pineapples, symbols of hospitality; according to Bosworth the gates were modeled on those at Hampton Court. The towering Oceanus Fountain commands the forecourt. The basic structure of the gardens dates from 1908, but the forecourt, Oceanus Fountain, headwall, and grand stair leading down to the three sculptures by George Grey Barnard were created when it became clear that the imposing facade of the second version of the house demanded a grander entrance court. The fill that was brought in and the sod cover at ground level are supported by a system of concrete vaults and coffers below.

The idea for the Oceanus Fountain was Bosworth's, as a letter from Jr. to JDR attests:

The eastern grand stair descends from the forecourt to a terrace. Set in a niche in the retaining wall is Barnard's marble sculpture Adam and Eve.

May 10, 1913
Dear Father,

In connection with the enlargement of the forecourt, Mr. Bosworth tells me that in his early talks with you he emphasized the fact that the central feature of the entire forecourt must be some large and commanding piece of sculpture. . . . Very probably you will remember his reference to this matter and that Mr. Platt [Charles Platt had designed the house and garden of Jr.'s sister Edith's Villa Turicum in Lake Forest, Illinois] fully agreed in Mr. Bosworth's opinion.

For a number of months, Mr. Bosworth has been studying to determine just what would be the thing for this place. He is convinced that nothing more splendid or appropriate could be suggested than the reproduction of a noted fountain in Florence, which would stand high above the ground and make a magnificent effect from the entrance of the house as one looks towards the east. (Rockefeller Archive Center)

Carved in Florence, the fountain's figures were modeled after Giambologna's *Oceanus and the Three Rivers*, completed in 1576 for the Boboli Gardens. Oceanus reigns over three figures personifying the three rivers of the ancient world, the Nile, the Ganges, and the Euphrates, as well as the three ages of man—youth, middle age, and old age. Each figure pours water from a ewer into the massive granite bowl below. More than 22 feet (6.7 meters) in diameter, this bowl was quarried and carved on Crotch Island near Stonington, Maine, and shipped by schooner to Tarrytown. Magnificent elms, transplanted when full grown, once shaded the forecourt. Boxwood brought in from "an old Tarrytown estate" and from Pennsylvania and Massachusetts prompted Jr. to consider naming the house Boxwood Court, Boxwood Manor, or simply Boxwood. "Thoroughly appropriate, not pretentious, but homey and pleasantly suggestive," he thought.

Gardens in the Beaux Arts style were often extensions of the architecture of the house, outdoor rooms with strong axial references to the site, and Kykuit's were no exception.

The installation of the Oceanus Fountain, July 1914. The Carrara marble figures were carved in Florence; the granite bowl was quarried on Crotch Island, Maine.

The vaulted ceiling of the teahouse is painted in the manner of Raphael's designs at the Villa Madama; the furniture was based on Pompeian models.

In the article about the Kykuit gardens that Bosworth wrote for the *American Architect*, he touched upon this concept as well as many other tenets of his design philosophy:

We think that to give it such a character it should contain water, the very life of a garden; variety, so achieved as not to disturb the feeling that each feature is a part of the whole and linked together with it. Shade, as well as sunshine; sequestered and obscure places, tempting one to explore them, as well as open exposures; points especially adapted from which to enjoy the best views; and places screened and sheltered, where one may get away from the view. Places to keep cool in, and places to sun oneself in; places to walk and places to sit; bird notes and running water for sounds, and the flowers and fruit trees for color, odor and taste; in fact all the senses should be appealed to in the ideal garden. And one must not forget the note of antiquity, never neglected by the Chinese. They will carefully incorporate some old tree stump, if nothing better offers to remind the passer-by of the

past and of his little moment of existence in which to enjoy nature to the utmost. But dominating all these various parts, the garden should express "unity for the sake of harmony and in the hope of beauty."

The inner, or walled, garden, just off the south porch, was originally two sunken lawns bordered by low box hedges and punctuated by fancifully clipped topiaries imported from Holland by the New York firm Wadley & Smythe; there were floral borders of white candytuft and yellow pansies in spring and snapdragons in late summer and fall. A stone teahouse at the eastern end recalls in its proportions the Loggia of the Muses at the sixteenth-century Villa Lante; Charles Platt adapted this structure for his well-known gardens in Brookline, Massachusetts, Faulkner Farm (1896) and The Weld (1901). For the teahouse Bosworth chose, or possibly designed, furniture after Pompeian models; the ceiling murals are based on those by Raphael for the Villa Madama on the outskirts of Rome. In front of the teahouse is a marble fountain, where water cascades from a scallop-shell basin into two levels of

The elaborate wisteria-covered arbor that once paralleled the linden allée.

pools with fanciful gilt-bronze fountain spouts in the form of aquatic creatures—sea horses, snails, frogs, crabs, and naiads —by artist François-Michel-Louis Tonetti; the water then flows into a rill with five bubbling jets (a sixth is now covered by a sculpture by Aristide Maillol). To the west of the inner garden an allée of European lindens leads to a classical temple built for a marble Aphrodite, once thought to be a work of the fourth century B.C. by the Athenian sculptor Praxiteles. Before the lindens matured, a barrel-vaulted, wisteria-covered latticework arbor paralleled them on the terrace to the west; it was adorned with carved panels illustrating the fables of seventeenth-century French poet and satirist Jean de La Fontaine.

The brook garden was created just beyond the south wall of the inner garden. A stream bordered by large, weathered stones and weeping cherries meanders from the mouth of a grotto, which was, as Bosworth described it, "constructed against an original ledge of rock. Water drips from stalactites in the roof, which were imported from Genoa for this purpose, and falls on an ancient bronze Chinese water drum, filling the air with low-toned music." Bronze Japanese temple lanterns installed in 1908 flank the path that leads from the brook to the tennis lawn (site of the original tennis court). A 1936 planting plan for the brook garden by Arthur A. Shurcliff listed close to sixty perennials and bulbs, including clematis and columbine, larkspur, lobelia, lady's slipper, wild sweet William, trillium, many varieties of lilies and violets, speedwell, and yarrow.

To the south and east of Kykuit, just behind the classical teahouse of the inner garden, is the morning garden. Designed as a winter garden, it is planted with evergreens such

A marble fountain after Donatello's Goose Boy *occupies the center of the circular garden, or rose garden. The evergreen maze was removed in 1916.*

as laurel and rhododendron. A quiet haven, it features a wading pool with a central fountain spout in the form of a playful putti by Tonetti. Overlooking the pool is a cipolin marble column that came to the gardens from the estate of Stanford White and has been capped with a stone sphere and a bronze Winged Victory, a facsimile of one found at Pompeii.

The hilltop site lent itself well to the terracing so central to Italian garden design. As Bosworth described it, "The general form of the hill was that of an oyster shell, flat only at the top, and hardly flat there." From the level of the house and the inner garden, terraces descend toward the Hudson; the gently rolling, tree-covered hills in the distance suggest that the boundaries of the property extend to the banks of the Hudson, when in fact the village and railroad lie between the estate and the river.

At the foot of the grand stair to the west of the house is the Orange Tree Terrace, once shaded by six large orange trees in wooden planters that were moved seasonally from the orangerie. Edging the terrace is a black iron railing of intricately entwined grapes and leaves by Tiffany. In a niche lined with coral and stalactites is a sculpture by Karl Bitter, *Goose Girl* (1914), commissioned for the gardens. On the next level are three pools, each lined with pebble dash in black-and-white concentric circles that accentuate the rippling of the water; rough-hewn steps of natural stone descend into the central pool, which is fed by water from a grotto. Violet and white cyclamen cover the stone bridges to each of the smaller pools, in which sixteenth-century sculptures of tritons blow on their shell-shaped horns. Tubs of jasmine once stood before the "graceful little summer houses [i.e., pavilions at either end of the terrace] with round windows recalling Chinese design." The stone steps to the lowest terrace are flanked by monumental figures of Hercules attributed to Orazio Marinali and dated to the late seventeenth century.

The rose garden, one of Abby Aldrich Rockefeller's favorites, is situated to the north of the house and can be viewed from the dining room and master bedroom above. When first designed, this garden was bordered by a double row of plane trees and had an evergreen maze in the northern quadrant. The maze was removed in 1916, and roses were planted there as well.

Jr. was pleased with the gardens and in the process of their design developed a lasting respect for Bosworth's taste and abilities. This led to his involving Bosworth in the design of the second version of Kykuit and the commissioning of the Oceanus Fountain as well as the three sculptures by George Grey Barnard. In 1911 Bosworth built the townhouse at 10 West Fifty-fourth Street in New York for Jr. and Abby. With Jr.'s backing, Bosworth designed the Egyptian Museum and Research Institute for James Breasted in 1923–25; the design was never realized, however. In 1922 he went to France, and in 1926 he was named secretary general of the Comité Franco-Américain pour la Restauration des Monuments. In this capacity he oversaw restoration projects at Versailles, Reims Cathedral, and Fontainebleau, all projects to which Jr. had contributed. For his work in France, Bosworth was honored with the Cross of the Commander of the Order of Arts and Letters and named a commander of the Legion of Honor. He remained in France until his death in 1966.

Six magnificent elms once shaded the forecourt and orange trees flanked the Oceanus Fountain, as seen in this 1920s photograph by Mattie Edwards Hewitt.

EVOLUTION

The 1930s and 1940s saw some changes in the gardens. In the early 1930s the barrel-shaped arbor was removed from the upper terraces. "Mr. Bosworth has replied to my letter about the large barrel shaped pergola in Father's gardens," Jr. wrote in 1932, "to the effect that he thinks the pergola is no longer needed since the double line of linden trees just back of it is now so fully grown." In the late 1930s, when Abby and Jr. were preparing to move into Kykuit, they commissioned the planting plan of the brook garden from Arthur A. Shurcliff, the Boston landscape architect who was deeply involved in the research and creation of many of the Colonial Revival gardens for the houses of Williamsburg at about the same time. In 1942 Bosworth and Jr. exchanged several letters on simplifying the main entrance of Kykuit. On October 5 Jr. wrote to Bosworth,

I wish we could arrive at some solution of the porte-cochere entrance garniture opposite the door that seems to disturb Mrs. Rockefeller but pleases me greatly as it always has. We have painted the flames of the two torches gray and they are much less challenging. Mrs. Rockefeller feels that the whole composition—the two torches, the granite coping that connects them, the large central vase between them and the two smaller vases that completed the picture but had been removed at her request—detracts from the stateliness and dignity of the facade of the building and seems fussy and busy. . . . In this connection one should speak of the two Foo dogs on the top of the steps, which are necessary, or something else if not they, in exactly those places to prevent a person falling off the top step.

On October 22, Bosworth replied,

As to the torches, they are really so fine (except for the glass flames, which could be modified; greatly subdued, if Mrs. Rockefeller wishes)—that every adjustment should be made to save them; especially as the marquise is so sumptuous, that it must be supported in richness by something 'en bas';— these torches are the only marble ones I know of (most reproductions of those Vatican candelabra are made in bronze). I don't mind confessing to you that I'm glad the lighting panel makes it all the more difficult to remove them!

Finally, on October 27 Jr. wrote,

It has been in my mind to suggest boxes covering entirely the four granite steps on which there stood the four smaller flower pots in the original composition. . . . The great objection to the scheme in my judgement is that anything done in wood in that important, central place would seem to me inadequate and unworthy. . . . The inevitable result would be, I fear, a letting down in preciousness of material and construction at the very center of the picture where the curve of preciousness should rise. . . . In light of your letters Mrs. Rockefeller is perhaps realizing a little more than she has heretofore the beauty and significance of the marble torches. She does see that the marquise calls for some important treatment. She also realizes, as she did not before, that the electric switchboards covering the garden lights are in these torches, which makes their removal all the more difficult, inconvenient and costly. (Rockefeller Archive Center)

In the end, the changes discussed were not carried out, and the arrangement of the torches and vases is today as it was originally designed by Bosworth in 1913. Besides the redesign of the golf course in 1934, the changes that Jr. and Abby made to the gardens were minimal.

When Nelson Rockefeller and his family moved into Kykuit in the early 1960s, one of his first modifications was the removal of the lattice arbor on the north side of the house toward the rose garden. It was replaced by a double row of English hornbeam leading from the house to the fountain in the center of the rose garden.

In the snowy winter of 1962–63 works by Aristide Maillol, Marino Marini, Elie Nadelman, and Gaston Lachaise were installed on the grounds, and works by Alberto Giacometti, Constantin Brancusi, and David Smith on the porches. Initially, advice was sought from friends, and Alfred Barr, Dorothy Miller, and René d'Harnoncourt offered suggestions on the installation. The first Museum of Modern Art garden had been installed in 1939, while Nelson was president of MoMA. Although he may not have been conscious of then-current museological theories on installation, he would have absorbed the basic tenets, which dictated that each piece be seen in its own space. His placement of sculpture at Kykuit reflects this precept. Swimming pools were placed in the sunken lawns of the inner garden, and several of the sculptures Nelson installed reflected the theme of bathing. Maillol's *Bather Putting Up Her Hair* (1930) graces the rill between the two pools. At the end of each pool stand works by the English sculptor Reg Butler—*Girl with a Vest* (1953–54) and *Manipulator* (1954). Nadelman's groups *Two Circus Women* (c. 1930, cast 1951) and *Two Female Nudes* (c. 1931, cast 1949) stand sentinel along the south wall, along with *Elevation* (1921–27, cast 1967) by Lachaise, *Torso: Chained Action* (c. 1906) by Maillol, and two abstract totemic pieces, *High Night* (1963) by Ezra Orion and *Barrier No. 1* (1962) by Robert Adams. Over the next fifteen years, new sculptures were added to the collection each season. By 1979 there were more than seventy works. International in scope, the collection is a reflection of the major trends in modern sculpture throughout the first three-quarters of this century, from the classicism of Maillol to the minimalism of Tony Smith and Clement Meadmore, from the whimsy of Alexander Calder to the monolithic work of Henry Moore, from the bimorphism of Jean Arp to the drawing in space of David Smith, from the assemblages of Picasso to the reductions of Brancusi.

THE JAPANESE GARDEN

The Japanese garden was originally designed in 1908 by Bosworth in collaboration with two Japanese landscape designers, Ueda and Takahashi, as a hill and pond garden, with a Meiji-style teahouse built of mahogany by master carpenters—much to the agitation of Jr., who had not been consulted on the choice of this expensive material. Letters refer to bamboo summer houses, but these did not last. Between 1880 and World War I garden design benefited from a tremendous influx of new botanical material, especially from Asia. A fascination with the exotic fostered the creation of Japanese gardens, an early example of which is the one planted on Isabella Stewart Gardner's estate in Brookline, Massachusetts, in 1885. In 1893 a Japanese garden was designed on an island at the World's Columbian Exposition in Chicago. Seven Springs, the home Charles Platt built in 1915–19 for Agnes and Eugene Meyer in Mount Kisco, New York, boasted a Chinese garden. In the early 1960s, just before Nelson came to Kykuit, the original teahouse was moved, and he commissioned Junzo Yoshimura to design a shoin-style teahouse; in 1954 and 1955 Yoshimura had designed a "House in the Garden" at MoMA for an exhibit, and this early contact may have been Nelson's inspiration for the teahouse, which was built in Kyoto by Nakamura Komuten and then assembled by craftsmen on site in the winter of 1962.

At the same time landscape artist David Harris Engel was commissioned to augment the garden. Engel had studied in Japan in the 1950s under Tansai Sano, a master landscape architect from Kyoto. A grove of densely planted bamboo was added on the upper slopes. An ocher stucco wall capped with gray-brown roof tiles extends along the western boundary, separating the garden from the open lawns of the golf course. Engel designed a garden for meditation—a dry landscape garden *(kare-sansui)* based on the fifteenth-century garden at the Zen temple Ryoan-ji in Kyoto. Five groups of rocks are arranged within the expanse of raked white gravel; they can be seen as islands in a vast sea or mountain peaks rising above banks of clouds or mist. Traditional stepping stones lead through the meandering stream and across a deep gorge, where carp once swam, past a twelve-foot-high water-

fall. A moss garden once covered the steep banks of the stream. Stones of many shapes and sizes form the pathways: cobblestones from an Albany street, smooth round river stones, and large and small squares of gray granite. Roof tiles placed on edge pave the path leading to an arched stone bridge. A millstone marks the spot where two paths diverge. Stone lanterns, pagodas, and water basins grace the paths. To the west of the pond in front of the teahouse are two conical piles of gravel; a low azalea hedge, clipped to mirror their shape, leads the eye to the rolling lawns and further to the distant cliffs across the Hudson; this illustrates clearly the Japanese design principle of *shakkei*, or "borrowed scenery." Engel's planting plan includes groves of Japanese red- and green-leaf maples, thread-leaf maple, andromeda, flame, scarlet, and white azaleas, flowering cherry, hemlock, hinoki cypress, white pine, mugho pine, rhododendron, mountain laurel, and dogwood. The cushions of verdant moss and gray-green lichen that cover the stone walls lend a soft patina of age—a quality prized in Japan as *sabi*.

The Kykuit gardens are significant for being among the few continuously maintained Beaux Arts gardens in the country. Their great and varied beauty was perhaps best expressed by William Welles Bosworth himself in *The Gardens of Kÿkuit* (1919):

> But to know this enchanting hill-top one must experience the early morning with its long shadows and dewy freshness, its fragrance, and the song of birds; or late evening when all is peacefully eloquent of aloofness from the busy world; when the glimmer of the lights of Tarrytown and Nyack far across the Tappan Zee lend a fairylike charm, enhanced now and then by the brilliant search lights from the river steamboats as they silently move along; or when moonlight caresses the marble statues and makes phosphorescent glint and glitter in the splashing fountains. The impressions left from these and countless similar experiences enrich the memories of those who know the gardens at "Kÿkuit."

Opposite: Commanding the forecourt is a magnificent replica of Giambologna's Oceanus and the Three Rivers *(1571–75); the original is in the Boboli Gardens in Florence. Oceanus towers over personifications of the Nile, Ganges, and Euphrates pouring water from ewers into the large granite basin. Above and below: A pair of urns modeled by Emil Siebern grace the forecourt lawns. Right: Torcheres of veined marble with flame-form globes of favrille glass flank the entryway.*

Top left: The ceiling of the teahouse, after Raphael's at the Villa Madama, features four oval panels of landscapes with cherubs, swans, cranes, sparrows, and doves, and a center roundel in relief of Venus in a shell-shaped chariot on the backs of two dolphins.
Bottom left: The classical stone teahouse, designed by Bosworth, forms the eastern boundary of the inner garden.

Above: The furniture is inspired by Pompeian and Roman models. The walls are ornamented with relief panels of dancing musicians, maidens, and fawns by Siebern.

Right: The inner garden. Conically shaped ever-greens and low box hedges, where once there were fanciful topiaries and elaborate floral borders, bring focus to the sculpture—works by Maillol, Nadelman, Lachaise, Adams, and Orion.

Above and right: The linden allée leads to a classical temple sheltering a marble Aphrodite, once thought to be a work of the fourth century B.C.

The brook garden. Along the rocky banks of the meandering stream are three sculptures of gabbro ("black granite"): on the pedestal is Black Sun *(1960–63) by Isamu Noguchi, a working model for the monumental work in Seattle; across from it are* Jubilee *(1965) and* Moonpath *(1967; not visible) by Japanese sculptor Masayuki Nagare.*

The morning garden. In the center of the shallow pool is a gilt-bronze fountain spout of a putti riding a sea creature by F.-M.-L. Tonetti. The cipolin column, one of several works that came to the gardens from the estate of Stanford White, is topped by a sphere and a nineteenth-century bronze Winged Victory.

The western terraces. Clockwise from top left: View of the putting green; detail of the iron and bronze Tiffany rail at the edge of the Orange Tree Terrace; on that terrace Karl Bitter's Goose Girl *(1914)* dances in a niche lined with coral and stalactites; snow covers the grand stair as it descends from the linden allée to Jacques Lipchitz's Song of Vowels *on the* Orange Tree Terrace to the grotto on the Swimming Pool Terrace.

The Swimming Pool Terrace consists of three pools "paved with black and white pebbles in decorative patterns and scallop shells . . . set in a row around the rim" (Bosworth). Many Rockefeller children learned to swim in the center pool (top right), which is the largest. Sixteenth-century Italian stone tritons grace each of the smaller pools (top left). Pavilions stand at either end of the terrace.

Left, top and bottom: A fanciful cast-stone mushroom-shaped table and stools are sheltered by a pergola on the level below the Swimming Pool Terrace. Above: Hercules and the Lion *(early eighteenth century), attributed to Orazio Marinali, is one of two marble figures brought to Pocantico from the Warwick, Rhode Island, estate of Abby's father, Senator Nelson W. Aldrich.*

The rose garden. Above: In the center is a fountain with a Goose Boy at the top. It was modeled after a Medici fountain ascribed to Donatello that is now in the Pitti Palace, Florence. Below: A single deep red bloom of the Mr. Lincoln hybrid tea. Right: The rose garden in full bloom, with borders of floribunda (Betty Prior, Gene Boerner), grandiflora (Queen Elizabeth, Love, and Caribbean) and hybrid teas (Miss All-American Beauty, Las Vegas, King's Ransom, American Spirit, American Pride, Mr. Lincoln, and John F. Kennedy).

Left, top and bottom: The grand stair to the east of the forecourt leads from the Oceanus Fountain to Adam and Eve *by George Grey Barnard.*

Above: Commissioned in 1916 and completed in 1923, this monumental composition joined two others by Barnard, Hewer *(1915), and* Rising Woman *(commissioned in 1915 and completed in 1918). Seven signs of the zodiac—Taurus through Scorpio—are depicted in a semicircular colored-stone mosaic in the pavement in front of* Adam and Eve.

Midway down the north end of the grand stair is the boxwood, or Italian, garden. It is heavily shaded by towering hemlocks, and moss and lichen line its paths. At the end is a replica (by Frederick Roth, commissioned for the gardens) of the Sleeping Ariadne in the Vatican collections. Each quadrant of the garden is graced with a cast-stone figure representing one of the seasons. Winter is seen here.

Left: In a sheltered niche of natural rock near the classical temple, a bronze Pan *by Janet Scudder pipes above a shallow pool.*

Opposite: Myriad mythical creatures and figures populate the gardens. Counterclockwise from top right: a gator spouts in a hexagonal well curb off the rose garden; a young monkey (by F.-M.-L. Tonetti) clings to a rocky wall near the tennis lawn; one of four singing visages on the marble vase-shaped fountain on the south porch; Orpheus (by Tonetti) fiddles in the linden allée; a wreathed bronze head at the horse trough near the parking area; the trireme pool, which once held water lilies, near the guest entrance; the head of Bacchus, near the tennis lawn; Eurydice (by Tonetti) among the cattails in a fountain in the forecourt; a gilt-bronze seahorse fountain spout in front of the classical teahouse (center).

The Japanese Garden. Opposite, far left: a view west across the pond; top left: tsukubai *(water basin), just in front of the teahouse; bottom left: moss and lichen cloak walls and steps, lending a patina of age. This page, above: the* kare-sansui *(dry landscape garden), modeled on the garden at Ryoan-ji in Kyoto; below:* ishi-doro *(stone lantern) and bamboo fence; top right: long afternoon shadows in the grove of Japanese maples; bottom right:* tobi-ishi *(stepping stones) across the cobblestone and pebble sea fork north and west.*

Left: The Japanese teahouse was designed by Junzo Yoshimura in 1961. The pond is fed by a stream that begins at the Oceanus Fountain in the forecourt. Above: A small stone frog basks in the sun at the edge of the pond.

There are shoji on all four sides of the teahouse.
A square stone wellhead can be seen in the garden
to the east. In the center of the twelve-mat tatami
room is a low lacquered table; on the left is the
tokonoma, where a scroll, a flower arrangement,
or treasured objects would be displayed.

Fusuma *(sliding doors) separate the two*
main spaces.

The southeast corner of the teahouse contains a
deep cedar tub overlooking a small walled garden.

Left, top and bottom: Whether cloaked in winter snow or autumn foliage, the thread-leaf maple on the hill between the Japanese garden and the lowest terrace of Kykuit's gardens is an elegant sight.

Above: The late afternoon sun illuminates a thread-leaf maple near the upper entrance to the Japanese garden.

Opposite, clockwise from top left: Stepping stones across the pond of the lower garden, a section remaining from the 1908 design; the Meiji teahouse is set deep in a grove of white pines; a Tibetan bronze of a monk is seated in front of a Tibetan painted scroll; sliding panels separate the teahouse's two rooms.

A gallery of the silent but watchful guardians of the gardens: The lion mask on the base of one of the Hercules sculptures.

One of the stern visages that emerge at each corner of the forecourt vases designed by Emil Siebern.

Flora smiles benignly from the keystone of the north gate in the forecourt's stone wall.

One of two rather fierce lion heads on the east terraces.

A snow-capped ancient face above the north arbor.

Bacchus's head, wreathed in grape leaves, peers through snowy vines beside the tennis lawn.

Above, left and right: Nineteenth-century cast-stone figures of Amphitrite, queen of the sea (left), and Apollo (right), from the Estate of Nelson W. Aldrich, Warwick, Rhode Island.

Opposite: Chant des Voyelles (Song of Vowels, *1931–32, this cast 1952–53) by Jacques Lipchitz is sited at the center of the Orange Tree Terrace overlooking the Hudson. Lipchitz titled this abstract depiction of two harpists after an Egyptian prayer composed only of vowels that was designed to subdue

the forces of nature. To the left are Spatial Concept: Nature I *and* Nature II *(1968, after terra-cottas of 1959) by Lucio Fontana, and to the right is Henry Moore's* Nuclear Energy *(1964–65), a working model for the twelve-foot-high sculpture at the University of Chicago.*

In the summer of 1966 Nelson commissioned Alexander Calder to make a large version of his twenty-six-inch-high stabile Spiny for the Kykuit gardens. The original, which had been displayed in the art gallery, was bequeathed to the Museum of Modern Art. Large Spiny was made under Calder's supervision at Etablissement Biemont in Tours, France; upon its arrival in the early summer of 1967 it was sited on a bank below the maple walk overlooking the Hudson and Palisades.

Picasso's The Bathers *(1956–57), at the edge of the tennis lawn, is one of two bronzes after the wood original now in the Staatsgalerie in Stuttgart. It is a whimsical work of assembled pieces: squat, vase-shaped legs from a bureau form the feet of the tall, slender* Woman Diver; *stretchers for canvases serve as the arms of* Man with Clasped Hands *and* Fountain Man; *broom and shovel handles nailed to planks create these planar figures.*

James Rosati's Lippincott II *(1965–69), of painted cor-ten steel, sits on the bank below the maple walk overlooking the Hudson. The irregular geometric forms stacked one upon another are animated by the tenuous nature of their joints.*

Alexander Liberman's Above II *(1973), of painted steel, is a striking sight against the bleached trunks of the copper beeches and the snow.*

In the inner garden, where swimming pools were installed in the 1960s for the children and grandchildren, several sculptures reflect the theme of bathing. Left: Gaston Lachaise's Standing Woman, or Elevation (1912–27, this cast 1967), is one of his many portraits of his wife, Isabel Nagle Lachaise. Right: Aristide Maillol's Bather Putting Up Her Hair (1930), after a small bronze of 1898.

On the south porch overlooking the inner garden is Elie Nadelman's Circus Woman I (c. 1924, this cast 1965). A photograph of a circus woman in just this pose was found in Nadelman's papers after his death. "I am particularly fond of Nadelman's sculpture," Nelson commented in Art in America, April 1965. "He was a curious and wonderful man. . . . What interests me in Nadelman, apart from the beauty and wit of his pieces, is his very democratic concept of making many of his sculptures in papier-mâché, with the idea that they would be more financially available to the public."

Girl with a Vest *(1953–54), a cast shell bronze by British sculptor Reg Butler, stands at the east end of the inner garden.*

Richard Fleischner's Girl on a Swing *(1966–67), of fiberglass, resin, and rope, is suspended from a maple at the edge of the tennis lawn.*

Henry Moore's Knife Edge—Two Piece
(1962; large version, 1965–66), suggests cliffs
of mountains, rocky coastlines, quarries, and the
thin "knife-edge of a breastbone."

Clement Meadmore's Double Up *(1975), of cor-ten steel, presides over the eastern edge of the golf course. "This one has caused me some trouble in the family," Nelson once remarked, "because it is rather large and there are those who feel that it has strayed on the place."*

The polished bronze surface of Peter Chinni's Natura Extensa *(1965) reflects the evening light.*

Crocus, *one of the five geometric shapes compris-ing* Wandering Rocks, *1967, by Tony Smith; the others are* Smohawk, Dud, Slide, *and* Shaft. *Nelson often rearranged their placement.*

Barbara (Hommage to Barbara Reise; *1971–72) by Benni Efrat. This composition of five square slabs of stone grooved to contain a cable is sited along the shaded maple walk.*

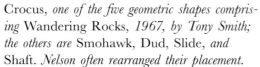

David Smith's The Banquet *(1951), steel,*
perches on the wall of the west porch. With its
floating images of fish, emblematic discs, and
folded metal forms, it is a drawing in space,
lyrical and full of movement.

Max Bill's Triangular Surface in Space *(1962), a geometric abstraction of polished rose granite on a gray granite column, early found its perfect site at the end of the rose garden pergola.*

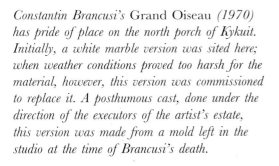

Constantin Brancusi's Grand Oiseau *(1970) has pride of place on the north porch of Kykuit. Initially, a white marble version was sited here; when weather conditions proved too harsh for the material, however, this version was commissioned to replace it. A posthumous cast, done under the direction of the executors of the artist's estate, this version was made from a mold left in the studio at the time of Brancusi's death.*

Gaston Lachaise's Man *(1930–35, cast 1938), at the edge of the putting green overlooking the newly clipped taxus and hemlock, is considered by some to be a combined portrait of ballet patron and writer Lincoln Kirstein and the artist's stepson, Edward Nagle.*

Marino Marini's Horse *(1951) is among the first sculptures brought to Kykuit in the winter of 1962–63. With head pulled back in a stance full of energy and tension, it stands just below the putting green.*

Above: The classical restraint of Night *(1902–9, this cast after 1944) by Aristide Maillol. In 1907, about the time this work was being created, but long before it graced the lawns at Kykuit, Jr. wrote to Abby: "This is a perfect night. . . . After a day and night of rain and mist and fog it has cleared off wonderfully, and the air is clear, a delicious breeze blows, the river is charming."*

Overleaf: Karel Appel's Mouse on Table *(1971), a whimsical nine-foot-high aluminum sculpture, has been placed in the children's garden to the east of the morning garden and classical teahouse.*

PHOTOGRAPHER'S NOTE

When my grandfather Nelson Rockefeller died in 1979, I was not prepared for the impact that his death would have on my family and me. Suddenly Kykuit was without the warm presence of family, and the idea of the National Trust owning the Big House and all the land surrounding it became a reality. There were rumors that the whole area would eventually become off-limits to the family. I soon began my own personal crusade to photograph all that would be lost to me. I wanted to be able to look at the images and remember every wonderful moment I had experienced there. It was my way of both holding on to and letting go of the past.

The more photographs I took, the harder it was to stop. I became determined to capture everything. While I was busy wandering about the property with my camera, my mother (Ann Roberts) and other family members began encouraging me to compile my photographs into a book. The idea slowly took shape. It was to be a book not just of pretty pictures but of all the different aspects of the estate at different times of day and year. I wanted it to be a personal view that also reflected the memories and thoughts of family members who had spent time there, so that the reader could get a feeling for what it had been like for each of the generations to live in this magnificent place. The perfect person to help in this endeavor was my mother. I loved her writing and knew that she would be able not only to capture the family's many different views and voices but also to weave them together with the history of the estate into a wonderful text. This book would not be complete without my mother's touch. I am most grateful for her patience and hard work.

Even though I started taking photographs in 1980, it was not possible to pursue the project seriously until the early 1990s, when Kykuit was leased to the Rockefeller Brothers Fund and was being prepared to open to the public.

I have used only natural light for the exterior shots and some minimal lighting when needed for the interiors. It has been wonderful photographing the place (especially taking the aerial shots) and recalling all the adventures I had there over the years. Being able to come to Kykuit as a child and roam around at will, with all the sculptures, gardens, and trails as a playground, was a great privilege; but I don't think I fully understood how truly unique my family's country home was until completing this book.

MARY LOUISE PIERSON
DECEMBER 1997

ACKNOWLEDGMENTS

Writing and photography are solitary pursuits in their execution but intensely cooperative in everything that precedes and follows them. The writing of this book was particularly illustrative of this truth. By virtue of its being a personal photographic essay and intimate history of one family's home, the understanding, guidance, and help of many were essential.

First has been the privilege, adventure, and pleasure of working with my daughter Mary Louise Pierson. It was her love of Pocantico that inspired her to take these photographs over a ten-year period while the estate was being readied to become public. Her invitation to me to write the introduction drew us together in this endeavor. She joins me in acknowledging all those who assisted us.

Many members of our family shared their memories of and feelings for Kykuit and the Pocantico Estate. We are most grateful to each of them for their willingness to open their hearts in this way so that visitors to Kykuit can have a deeper understanding of our family life as we grew up in and around Pocantico. David Rockefeller, Laurance Rockefeller, and Happy Rockefeller gave wonderful interviews, sharing material that would not have been available otherwise. David generously allowed Mary Louise unlimited access to his chartered helicopter for the aerial shots. Many fourth-, fifth-, and sixth-generation members came forward to talk with us and contributed fine stories, a number of which are in the book. Among the fourth-generation members who shared their reminiscences most generously are: Abby M. O'Neill, Rodman C. Rockefeller, Steven C. Rockefeller, David Rockefeller Jr., Marion R. Weber, Eileen and Paul Growald, Nelson A. Rockefeller Jr., and Mark Rockefeller; among the fifth and sixth: Peter C. Rockefeller, Gail Caulkins, Joseph A. Pierson, Rachel Gumina, Ingrid Rockefeller, Jennifer R. Nolan, Steven C. Rockefeller Jr., Sabrina R. Donahue, and Naomi F. Waletzky, Space would not permit the inclusion of all the stories; time, the gathering of many more yet untold, but all the voices played a part in the book's unfolding.

The Rockefeller Archive Center and the files at Kykuit and the Greenrock Corporation were the principal sources for our research. At the Archive Center Dr. Darwin Stapleton, Tom Rosenbaum, and Michele Hiltzik were most helpful in directing us in our search for relevant materials and historical family photographs. The staff at Greenrock was always ready to assist us. Special thanks to Patricia Higgins, Greenrock's Director of Special Events and Personal Services. Thanks also to the grounds crew at Kykuit for helping Mary Louise with specific shots.

Charles L. Granquist, Director of Pocantico Programs for the Rockefeller Brothers Fund, was instrumental in convincing us to pursue this project. Cynthia B. Altman, Curator of the Kykuit Collections, not only guided and supported the research for the book but also wrote the introductions to the photographic sections and the captions with great erudition and grace. Peter Johnson, the co-author of two books on the Rockefeller family, was always ready to answer odd questions and solve factual riddles. He also was kind enough to read the final text, along with Cynthia Altman, my sister, Mary Callard, and others. Dorothy Bronson, Mary Kresge, Oscar Ruebhausen, and Joe Canzeri offered invaluable recollections of family members and times at Kykuit. Ruth Kuhlman and her excellent staff at the Rockefeller family offices saw to several important practical matters. My assistant, Loislee Giambri, was there at every turn to help expedite the process.

Ann Parker, photographer and author of many books, and her husband, Avon Neal, mentored Mary Louise throughout this project, helping her to develop and refine her photographic skills. Mary Louise is very grateful to Ann for her expertise and very positive guidance.

Mary Louise would also like to thank her husband, Jamie Wert, and her daughter, Raven, for their patience from start to finish.

Special thanks to John Dobkin, President of Historic Hudson Valley, who encouraged us to take the project to Abbeville Press. Mary Louise and I feel blessed in having Abbeville as our publisher. We have been supported every step of the way. Our editor, Jackie Decter, has worked with infinite patience, skill, and sensitivity to bring the book together, as has our designer, Patricia Fabricant.

ANN ROCKEFELLER ROBERTS
MARY LOUISE PIERSON
DECEMBER 1997

VISITOR'S GUIDE

A property of the National Trust for Historic Preservation, Kykuit is maintained and administered by the Rockefeller Brothers Fund (RBF), by agreement with the National Trust. The RBF operates the site as a center for its philanthropic programs. Historic Hudson Valley, a network of museum properties founded in 1951 as Sleepy Hollow Restorations by John D. Rockefeller Jr., administers the visitation program.

Kykuit is open to the public from May through October, six days a week. It is closed on Tuesdays.

To reach the Kykuit visitor center at nearby Philipsburg Manor by car: from the New York Thruway, take exit 9 and drive 2 miles north on Route 9; from I-95, the Hutchinson River Parkway, or the Merritt Parkway, take I-287 West and follow signs to the Thruway. Philipsburg Manor is also accessible by train: from Grand Central Station in New York City, take the Metro North railroad to the Tarrytown station.

For reservations or further information, please call (914) 631-9491.

BIBLIOGRAPHY

BOOKS AND MANUSCRIPTS

Bearss, Edwin C. Untitled manuscript on the Pocantico Hills Estate, early 1970s (Rockefeller Archive Center).

Berger, Albert I. "Kykuit Design and Construction, 1902–1915: Time Line and Summary of Correspondence," unpublished manuscript, 1984 (Rockefeller Archive Center).

———. "My Father's House at Pocantico Hills: Kykuit and the Business Education of JDR, Jr.," unpublished manuscript, 1985 (Rockefeller Archive Center).

Bosworth, William Welles. *The Gardens of Kijkuit*, privately printed, 1919.

Chase, Mary Ellen. *Abby Aldrich Rockefeller*. New York: The Macmillan Company, 1950.

Day, Paula, and Tom Pyle. *Pocantico: Fifty Years on the Rockefeller Domain*. New York: Sloan & Pearce, 1964.

Fosdick, Raymond B. *John D. Rockefeller, Jr.: A Portrait*. New York: Harper & Brothers, 1956.

Harr, John Ensor, and Peter Johnson. *The Rockefeller Century: Three Generations of America's Greatest Family*. New York: Charles Scribner's Sons, 1988.

———. *The Rockefeller Conscience: An American Family in Public and in Private*. New York: Charles Scribner's Sons, 1991.

Kert, Bernice. *Abby Aldrich Rockefeller: The Woman in the Family*. New York: Random House, 1993.

Lieberman, William S. *Twentieth Century Art from the Nelson Aldrich Rockefeller Collection*. New York: Museum of Modern Art, 1969.

McCauley, Hugh J., AIA United Architects. "The Pocantico Historic Area, National Historic Landmark Survey and Historic Structures Report of John D. Rockefeller's Estate at Pocantico Hills," unpublished manuscript, 1994.

Miller, Dorothy Canning, ed. *The Nelson A. Rockefeller Collection: Masterpieces of Modern Art*. New York: Hudson Hills Press, 1981.

Nevins, Alan. *John D. Rockefeller: The Heroic Age of American Enterprise*. New York: Charles Scribner's Sons, 1940.

Roberts, Ann Rockefeller. *Mr. Rockefeller's Roads: The Untold Story of Acadia's Carriage Roads and Their Creator*. Camden, Maine: Down East Books, 1990.

Rockefeller, Abby Aldrich. *Abby Aldrich Rockefeller's Letters to Her Sister Lucy*. John D. Rockefeller Jr., ed. New York: privately printed, 1957.

Rockefeller, John D. *Random Reminiscences of Men and Events*. Tarrytown: Sleepy Hollow Press and the Rockefeller Archive Center, 1984.

ARTICLES AND TRANSCRIPTS

Bosworth, William Welles. "The Garden at Pocantico Hills, Estate of John D. Rockefeller, Esq." *American Architect* 99 (January 4, 1911): 1–12.

"The Country Home of John D. Rockefeller, Esq." *The House Beautiful* 26 (June 1909): 1–9.

du Plessix, Francine, "Anatomy of a Collector: Nelson Rockefeller." *Art in America*, April 1965, 27–46.

"John D. Rockefeller's Pocantico Estate." *The Country Calendar* 1 (November 1905): 633–37.

Rockefeller, Nelson A. "The Governor Lectures on Art." *New York Times Magazine*, April 9, 1967.

———. "1977 Arts Award Presentation of the Council for the Arts in Westchester," December 16, 1977. Transcript and audio tape (Rockefeller Archive Center).

Saarinen, Aline. "The One Luxury: The Rockefellers." In *The Proud Possessors*. New York: Random House, 1958, pp. 344–95.

———. "The Art of Collecting," January 19, 1964. Transcript (Rockefeller Archive Center).

INDEX

Page numbers in *italics* refer to illustrations.

Abeyton Lodge, 14, 19, 21, 22, 101
Adams, Robert, 144, *149*
Aldrich, Chester H., 15, 54
Aldrich, Lucy, 25, 43
Aldrich, Ned, 102
Alpuy, Julio, 59
Ames, Joseph Alexander, 58, *80*
Appel, Karel, 58, *186–87*
Armstrong, Louis, 42
Arp, Jean, 144
art gallery at Kykuit, 30, 59, *86–89*
automobile collection, 98–99, *112–13*

Balla, Giacomo, *91*
Barnard, George Grey, 102, 103, *129*, 139, *140*, 143, *156*
Barr, Alfred, 144
Bartley, Anne, 51
Bass, Robert M., 47
Baumgarten, William, 56
Beaux Arts design, 15, 54, 140
Bill, Max, *182*
Bitter, Karl, 142, *152*
bodhisattva statue, 49, *78*
Bonnard, Pierre, *83*
Bontecou, Lee, 59
Bosworth, William Welles, 15, 17, 18, 23, 54, 98–100, 139–45
Brancusi, Constantin, 144, *183*
Brooks, James, 58
Buden, Clare Marie Pierson, 49
Burnham, Hitchings, Pierson, 99
Butler, Reg, 144, *177*

Calder, Alexander, 144, *172*
Campbell, Colin, 47
Candler, Duncan, 28, 98, 101, 103
Canzeri, Joe, 35, 37, 39
carriage collection, 98, *108*, *109*
cars and driving, 27, 39–40, 98–99, *99*, *108*, *112*, *113*

Cézanne, Paul, *83*
Chagall, Marc, 34, *87*
Chinni, Peter, *179*
Cinque, John, 45
Coach Barn, 13–14, 26–27, 38, 39, *39*, 45, 46, 47, 96–99, *96*, *97*, *104–13*
Codman, Ogden, 54, 55–57
Compston, Archie, 44
Cotton, Henry and Nora, 28

Davis, Meyer, 42
Degas, Edgar, *83*
Delano, William A., 15, 54
Delano & Aldrich, 15, 17, 18, 98
Dickinson, Edwin, 101, *123*
Donatello, *142*, *155*
Duchin, Peter, 34
Dunn, Jones Willie, 14
Dürrbach, J. de la Baume, atelier, 59, *88–89*
Duveen, Joseph, 57

Efrat, Benni, *180*
Eileson, Jorge, 59
Engel, David Harris, 40–41, 145
Evans, Mrs. Fannie A., 19
Eyrie (Seal Harbor, Maine), 101–2

Farrand, Beatrix, 102
Fleischner, Richard, *177*
Ford, Gerald, 33, 45
Forest Hill (Cleveland, Ohio), 9–10, 12, 139
Fosdick, Harry Emerson, 23
Fosdick, Raymond, 23
Fox, Virgil, 19, 23

Gabino, Amadeo, *86*
gardens at Kykuit, *26*, *68*, *121*, 139–87, *141*, *142*, *149*, *150*, *152*, *157;* design of, 15–16, 17, *17*, 40–41, 55, 101–3, 139–45; map of, *138;* sculpture in, *168–70*, *172–82*, *184–86.* *See also* Japanese garden; rose garden; terraces

Giacometti, Alberto, 144
Glarner, Fritz, 59
golfing and golf courses, 14, 19, 43–44, 144, *152*
Goodman, Benny, 42
Goodwin, Philip Lippincott, 101
Grotto, *90–91*
Growald, Eileen McGrath Rockefeller, 48
Growald, Paul, 49
Guastavino, *90*
Gumina, George, 49

Hamot, M., *79*
Harnoncourt, René d', 31
Harrison, Wallace K., 42, 103
Hartigan, Grace, 59, *86*
Hawes House, 33, 37
Herbert S. Newman & Partners, 50
Herter, Adele, 58
Higgins, Edward, 59, *86*
Historic Hudson Valley (HHV), 48
Hoppner, John, *80*
horses and riding, *25*, 26–27, *28*, *39*, 96–98, *109–11*

Japanese garden, *38*, 40–41, *40*, 46, *65*, 144–45, *160–67*
Johnson, Philip, 30

Kaendler, Johann Joachim, 58
Kemény, Zoltan, 35, 58
Kent House, 14, 18
King, McKenzie, 23
Kirchner, Johann Gottlieb, 58
Kissinger, Henry, 34, 44
Komuten, Nakamura, 145
Kruger, Louise, *86*
Kykuit (Big House), 54–93; construction, *16;* costs, 11–12, 16–18; design and redesign, 17–18, 54; façades, *18*, *19*, 54, *64*, *66*, *67;* gates and forecourt, 18, *62*, *63*, *139*, *140*, *146;* interiors, *54*, 55–59, *55*, *69–72*, *75–85*, *92;* map of grounds,

138; preparation for public access, 47, 50; siting and plan of, 11–18, 54, *60;* National Trust, 45–51
Kykuit Hill, 10–11, *13*, 49

Lachaise, Gaston, 144, *149*, *176*, *184*
Lakewood House (Ocean County, N.J.), 14
Lanin, Lester, 42
Lassaw, Ibram, 58, 59
Lawrence, Sir Thomas, 58
Léger, Fernand, *86*
Liberman, Alexander, *175*
Lipchitz, Jacques, *152*, *171*
Lipton, Seymour, 59
Lytle, Richard, 59

Maillol, Aristide, 144, *149*, *176*, *185*
Mallary, Robert, 59
Manning, Warren, 11, 13, 139
Marinali, Orazio, 143, *154*
Marini, Marino, 144, *184*
Marisol, 59
Martin, David, 58, *70*
Martin, Mary, 25
Meadmore, Clement, 144, *179*
Mexican Arts Corporation, 103
Miller, Dorothy, 59, 144
Milliken, Henry Oothout, 101
Milton, David, 22
Milton, Marilyn, 22
Miró, Joan, 30, 34, 35, 58, *74*
Moore, Henry, 37, 144, *178*
Moravian Tileworks, *90*
Morgan, J. P., 57
Motherwell, Robert, 59
Museum of Modern Art, 29, 48, 103, 144, 145

Nadelman, Elie, 144, *149*, *176*
Nagare, Masayuki, *150*
Nanteuil, Robert, *71*
National Trust for Historic Preservation, 45–51

Negret, Edgar, 59
Nevelson, Louise, *87*
Noguchi, Isamu, *150*
Nolan, Jennifer Rasmussen Rockefeller, 50

Oceanus Fountain, *68*, 139–40, *140*, 143, *143, 146, 156*
Ogden, Peter, 30
Okada, Kenzo, 58
Olmsted, Frederick Law, 101, 139
O'Neill, Abby Milton (Mitzi), 19, 22, 25, 28, 42, 49
O'Neill, Wendy Harrison, 44
Orangerie, 46, 99–101, *100, 114, 115*
Orion, Ezra, 144, *149*

Paine, Frances Flynn, 103
painting collection, 58–59
Parsons–Wentworth House, 11, 12, *12*, 14, 98
Picasso, Pablo, 59, *87, 88–89*, 144, *173*
Pierson, Joseph A., 38, 40, 50
Pierson, Mary Louise, 37, 40–41
Pierson, Rachel Ann, 38, 40–41, 49
Platt, Charles, 98, 141, 145
Playhouse, 28–29, 41–43, 46, 51, 101–3, *116–20;* interiors, *122–33*
Plick, Joe and Julia, 26–27
Pocantico Conference Center, 47–51
Pocantico, *10, 11;* land acquisition, 9–13; the outbuildings, 96–135; willed to the National Trust, 45–51. *See also* Kykuit
Pocantico Historic Area, 46–47
Polesello, Rogelio, 59
porcelain collections, 57–58, *69, 71, 73, 74*
Pratt, J. B., *84*
Prentice, Parmalee and Alta Rockefeller, 14, 99
Pyle, Tom, 28

Raphael, 141, *141, 148*

Roberts, Ann Clark Rockefeller, 40
Rockefeller, Abby (Babs), 22, 29, 42, 47
Rockefeller, Abby Aldrich, 13, *15, 19*, 20–25, *24, 25*, 29, 33, 43, *85*, 99, 101, 103, 143; and design of estate, 101, 103
Rockefeller, Allison, 49
Rockefeller, Blanchette, 22
Rockefeller, David, 20, 21, 22, *28*, 29, 33, 37, 42, 43, 46, 47, 48, 99, 101
Rockefeller, David, Jr., 23, 24, 25, 27, 44, 46, 47, 51
Rockefeller, Eliza Davison, *14*
Rockefeller, Ingrid Rasmussen, 44, 45, 49
Rockefeller, John D. (JDR), *21, 23*, 46; acquisition of land, 9–13; anniversary commemoration, 48, 49; design and building of estate, 11–18, 139; life at Kykuit, 18–21, 39, 96; New York house at 4 West 54th St., 10, 55, 103, 143; personal character, 11–13, 17, 19–20
Rockefeller, John D., Jr. (Jr.), 9–14, 20, *25*, 34, 43, 46, 48; collecting by, 102; design and building of estate, 15–18, 43, 54, 56–57, 100, 101, 103, 139, 143, 145; life at Kykuit, 19, 21–29, 39, 96, 101, 143
Rockefeller, John D., 3rd, 22, 29, 42, 43
Rockefeller, Laurance, 20, 22, 29, 31, 33, 35, 39, 42, 43–44, 46, 47
Rockefeller, Laura Spelman, 9, 11, 13, 18
Rockefeller, Margaret McGrath (Peggy), 22, 48
Rockefeller, Margaretta Fitler (Happy), 29, 31, 33–34, 35, 38, 41, 45, 46, 47, 48
Rockefeller, Mark, 31–33, 39, 40, 44, 45
Rockefeller, Martha Baird Allen, 29, 42

Rockefeller, Mary French, 22, 43–44
Rockefeller, Mary Todhunter Clark, 22, 41
Rockefeller, Michael Sorum, 45
Rockefeller, Nelson A.: art collection, 30, 32, 34–37, 38, 41, 45, 58–59, 99; design and building of estate, 103, 139, 145; life at Kykuit, 22, 29–45, 144; National Trust bequest, 45–46
Rockefeller, Nelson, Jr., 31–33, 35, 38, 39, 43–44, 45
Rockefeller, Peter Clark, 37, 40, 45, 49
Rockefeller, Rodman Clark, 24, 25, 37
Rockefeller, Steven Clark, 37, 46, 51
Rockefeller, Steven Clark, Jr., 43–44
Rockefeller, William, 10, 11, 14
Rockefeller, Winthrop, 22, *28*, 29, 42, 98
Rockefeller Archive Center, 42
Rockefeller Brothers Fund (RBF), 47–48, 50
Rockefeller family: family tree, *6–7;* gatherings at Kykuit, 28, 34, 42, 48–50; group portraits, *8, 20, 22–24, 29–33, 36;* latest generations, 28, 37–38, 44–46, 48, 49, 50
Rockefeller Foundation, 48, 103
Rockwood Hall (William Rockefeller mansion), 10
Rodin, Auguste, 58
Rosati, James, *174*
rose garden, *60*, 143, *155*
Roth, Frederick, *157*
Rowe, Fred, *28*
Ruebhausen, Oscar, 34

Salisbury, Frank O., 58, *76*, 101, *123*
Sargent, John Singer, 58, *77*
Scudder, Janet, *158*

sculpture collection, 35–37, 102, 144, *168–70, 172–82, 183, 184–86*
Seley, Jason, 59
Seo, Helen, 41
Shurcliff, Arthur A., 101, 102, 142, 143
Siebern, Emil, *90, 147, 148, 168*
Smith, David, 144, *181*
Smith, Tony, 144, *180*
Smythe, Frederick, 100–102
Somaini, Francesco, *87*
Soria, Salvador, *87*
Soulages, Pierre, 58
Stevens House, 37
Strawbridge, Sabrina Vaux, 38
Stuart, Gilbert, 58, *79*
swimming pools, 27, 31, 42–43, *128, 129, 134*

Taggart, William, 39
teahouse, classical, 31, *141, 148*
teahouse, Japanese, *40*, 41, 145
tennis courts, 31, 103, *135*
terraces, 142, *152–54*
Tiffany Studios, 54, 56, *90*, 142, *152*
Tomlin, Bradley Walker, 58, *75*
Tonetti, François–Michel–Louis, 54, 142, *151, 159*
Toomey & Flynn, 43

Ueda and Takahashi, 145
Uht, Carol, 37

Wadley & Smythe, 100, 101, 141
Walter, J. Jackson, 47
Warhol, Andy, 34, *86*
Weber, Marion French Rockefeller, 43
Wharton, Edith, 55
Wheeler, Dunham A., 14–15

Yordi, Mr., 19
York & Sawyer, 13, 98
Yoshimura, Junzo, 41, 145

Zorn, Anders, 58, *75*